Improving Schools in Exceptionally Challenging Circumstances

Improving Schools Series

Series editors: Alma Harris and Jane McGregor

How to Improve your School – Jean Rudduck with Julia Flutter

Leading Teachers – Helen Gunter

Improving Schools in Difficulty – Paul Clarke (Editor)

Improving Schools Through Collaborative Enquiry – Hilary Street and Julie Temperley (Editors)

Improving Schools through External Intervention – Chris Chapman

School Improvement – Martin Thrupp

Improving Schools in Exceptionally Challenging Circumstances

Tales from the Frontline

Alma Harris, Judith Gunraj,
Sue James, Paul Clarke and Belinda Harris

continuum
LONDON • NEW YORK

Continuum International Publishing Group
The Tower Building
11 York Road
London
SE1 7NX

15 East 26th Street
New York
NY 10010

www.continuumbooks.com

British Library Cataloguing-in-Publication Data
A catalogue record for this book is available from the British Library.

ISBN: 0–8264–7494–2 (hardback)
        0–8264–7495–0 (paperback)

Typeset by Fakenham Photosetting Ltd, Fakenham, Norfolk
Printed and bound in Great Britain by MPG Books Ltd, Bodmin, Cornwall

This book is dedicated to the memory of James Learmonth
who was to be a co-author on this book until his untimely death in
2003. James was a champion of schools in difficult circumstances and
in his research and his professional life he was committed to social
justice and educational excellence for all young people.
While he is sadly missed by friends and colleagues, his firm belief that
schools make a difference continues.

Contents

Foreword

Schools in disadvantaged communities continue to present a problem to policy-makers in England and many other countries. Across such schools academic performance is well below the national norm and this is a pattern that persists. It is also clear that, for these schools, poverty presents a substantial barrier to educational attainment and achievement. As Gray (2000, p. 7) notes: 'Schools drawing their pupils from the least favoured socio-economic groups account for only 17% of schools throughout this country but the same data indicates that over two-thirds of failing schools belong to this group.' Data also shows that secondary schools in special measures have more than twice as many pupils on free school meals as the national average. Consequently, the link between socio-economic deprivation and the likelihood that the school will be found to be failing remains particularly strong.

School effectiveness research has consistently shown that between 8 and 15 per cent of the attainment difference between schools is accounted for by what they actually do, i.e. their internal conditions, rather than by their intake variations. In short, socio-economic context is a large and indisputable force that shapes the aspirations and subsequent attainment of young people in disadvantaged areas. However, despite the recognition of the 'profoundly close relationship between poverty and attainment' (Lupton 2004, p. 1), this has generally been factored out of attempts to improve schools in disadvantaged areas. The dominant policy response has been to suggest that it is a problem which is internal to the school and as a result many of the improvement programmes and initiatives have simply failed to grapple with the broader contextual issues. This has meant successive disappointments for many of the externally funded improvement programmes and projects aimed at raising achievement in the poorest schools.

While there are inevitable difficulties associated with embracing a more contextually focused approach to school improvement, it would seem imperative to do so to avoid replicating past failures. The reluctance to tailor school improvement policies to particular contexts is in part explained by a fear that it could be used to explain and excuse poor practice (Lupton 2004, p. 4). In other words, by dealing with issues that are external to the school there is a risk that poor teaching might be ignored. While this is a contested issue, it remains the case

that many approaches to improving schools in difficulty have concentrated upon fixing the problems within the school while ignoring the
broader contextual factors that compound these problems. The OCTET
project represented a departure from this trend. It was very clearly and
deliberately a school improvement project that was contextually driven
and designed to engage with the socio-economic issues facing schools in
exceptionally challenging circumstances. It set out to develop, refine and
test a model of intervention and improvement aimed at schools in some
of the most difficult socio-economic contexts in England.

As an innovative and developmental programme, the OCTET project
took its main theoretical stance from the school improvement research
field, but differed from previous school improvement projects in two ways.
First, although there were some core components of the programme, the
broad programme design evolved through interaction and negotiation
with the schools. There was no initial blueprint for change but it was
intended that the programme would respond to individual school
need. The absence of a template meant that adjustments, refinements
and changes to the programme could be made as it evolved, and that
contextual factors could be taken into account. Second, a focus on only a
few schools is a significant departure from previous school improvement
programmes, which have tended to operate on a much larger scale.
The concentration on just eight schools in 'exceptionally challenging
circumstances' meant that unlike larger scale interventions, the project
could engage more deeply with the process of change and development
and could look more closely at contextual influences. Unlike large-
scale interventions, the OCTET project was more able to explore how
improvement could be secured and what worked for schools in very
different contexts.

Within the school improvement field not only do we have few in-depth
accounts of change and development in schools in difficult circumstances
but also, where they do exist, these accounts have been chiefly compiled
and written by researchers or evaluators. Very rarely are the voices of
those on the frontline of change heard in the many descriptions of the
various programmes and projects around the world aimed at improving
schools in difficulty. Consequently, this book aims to give an insight into
the processes and practices of school improvement from the perspective of
those who experienced it most directly and acutely, the headteachers. Their
accounts of the OCTET project and its impact upon their school provide a

powerful insight into the way in which innovation and contextual factors collide. The honesty and tenacity of the heads in the OCTET project is apparent throughout their accounts of the process of change.

It is evident from these 'heads' tales' that context matters and that it is the single most powerful influence on a school's ability to improve. This must signal to the school improvement community the urgent need for more refined, contextually specific forms of intervention and development that originate from new knowledge about how schools in difficult circumstances improve. Looking at the field, many of the current models of school improvement tend to be reinvented or reconstituted models from a previous age that still fail to adequately address contextual issues. In this respect, the school improvement field is in danger of reaching a 'cul-de-sac' of development unless new knowledge is generated from working in an experimental and developmental way with networks of schools in different contexts and in different cultural settings.

It is clear that schools can and do make a difference to the life chances of young people and that some schools in difficult circumstances are better at achieving this than others. It is also clear that external support and additional resources can unlock the capacity for schools in the most difficult circumstances to succeed against the odds. While it is inevitable that, in the long run, broader social policies will contribute more to reducing attainment differences than any educational intervention or school improvement programme, it does at least give us a place to start while we wait.

ALMA HARRIS and JANE McGREGOR

References

Gray, J. (2000) *Causing Concern but Improving: A Review of Schools' Experiences*. London: Department for Education and Skills.

Lupton, R. (2004) *Schools in Disadvantaged Areas: Recognising Context and Raising Performance*. CASE paper 76, London: Centre for Analysis and Exclusion, London School of Economics and Political Science.

Acknowledgements

We are grateful to the OCTET schools and the DfES for giving us permission to publish this book. We would also like to thank all the teachers we worked with during the OCTET project and to acknowledge the other core members of the training team: Anne Allsop, Paul Buck, David Reynolds, Pat O' Brien and Phil Vaughan. While the work of many researchers within the school improvement and effectiveness field is represented in this book, we would like to acknowledge Professor John Macbeath and his Cambridge Evaluation team and Dr Christopher Chapman. Their work has contributed to our thinking and writing about schools in difficulty. A particular thank you is reserved for Louisa Hopkins for all her efforts on the final manuscript, and we are grateful to Alexandra Webster and Christina Parkinson from Continuum Publishing for their patience and support.

Part 1
Context Is All

1 Setting the Scene

Introduction

Across many countries, economic, social and political forces have amalgamated to produce a climate in which schools feel continued pressure to improve and to raise levels of achievement. The dominant educational reform agenda also reflects urgent attention to the issue of improving schools in the most difficult or disadvantaged circumstances. The issue of 'under-achievement' is high on the political agenda in the USA, Canada and England as it remains clear that certain groups of pupils in schools in disadvantaged contexts consistently fail to reach their potential while other groups of pupils in more affluent contexts consistently succeed. Recent research has shown that children from low-income families do not on average overcome the hurdle of lower initial attainment. It also highlights that class differences affect children long before they start school, and have a growing influence as they get older. The odds, it would seem, are 'still stacked against schools in poorer areas' and the social class differential remains a powerful indicator of subsequent educational achievement (Gray 2000, p. 1).

In England, successive governments have sought to sever the link between disadvantage and underachievement through policy-making aimed at structural intervention to generate a more equitable educational system. Circular 10/65 aimed to provide 'equality of opportunity' within a comprehensive school system that was designed to ameliorate class disadvantage. It formed a key moment in the constituting of the social democratic settlement that pursued social justice based on redistribution. An age of 'professional knowledge', it was suggested, would deliver the good society for its clients. Taking up the perspective of the National Commission of Education (1996), New Labour promoted the belief that good schools can defy expectations and 'succeed against the odds'. The NCE report argued that 'taking account of these factors [of disadvantage] shows that there is plenty of scope for the school to make a difference. Schools with similar intakes do not promote the progress of their pupils at the same rate' (NCE 1996).

Almost a decade earlier, the school effectiveness movement had reinforced the same point: the relative effectiveness of the school is a significant variable in subsequent educational attainment (Reynolds 1986). In its White Paper, *Excellence in Schools* (DfEE 1997), the Government argued that processes of improving standards mattered more than structures. It noted that 'The preoccupation with school structure has absorbed a great deal of energy to little effect. We know what it takes to create a good school' (DfEE 1997, p. 6). A further seven years on, in July 2004 Labour launched its Five Year Strategy for Children and Learners which acknowledges the need for change, in the context of transformations in society and economy and the realization that 'we have not yet broken the link between social class and achievement. No society can afford to waste the talent of its children and citizens.' It would seem that the bond between social class and educational achievement remains a particularly powerful and highly resistant one.

There remains interest at the highest policy levels in generating and sustaining improvement in 'low performing'[1] schools and an increased impetus to raise student achievement in schools in the most economically deprived areas. The Government has set itself and schools very ambitious targets. Reaching these targets is proving particularly difficult for schools located in areas of acute disadvantage. Although certain schools have been able to cross this achievement threshold, many more schools in areas of socio-economic disadvantage are simply not making the progress expected of them. In a recent Annual Report, the Chief Inspector notes that the gap between the average achievement in the highest performing schools and the lowest continues to widen (Ofsted 2003, paragraph 79). He also notes that 'the improvement in schools with the highest levels of social disadvantage has been greater than that of any group of schools'. It appears therefore that the negative relationship between deprivation, disadvantage and achievement prevails.

A substantial international corpus of research[2] into the nexus between poverty and education demonstrates that, while the attainment levels of poor children have increased over time, the gap between the majority of children from low-income families and their more affluent peers persists throughout schooling. It is clear that schools in disadvantaged areas

---

1 This is a fraught and contested concept, but is used here to denote the way it is conceived in policy.

2 There are indeed decades of evidence in the UK (e.g. Rutter, Mortimore and Maugham 1979; Smith and Noble 1995); Australia (e.g. Henderson 1975; Teese and Polesal 2003); and the USA (e.g. Apple 1982; Rainwater and Smeeding 2003).

perform below the national norm and that these patterns of performance are long and well established. In short, the more socially disadvantaged the community served by the school, the more likely it is that the school will appear to underachieve. Research also shows the cumulative effect of attending less effective schools. As Gray (2004, p306) points out, part of being disadvantaged seems to be about having the misfortune to end up attending 'poorer' institutions than chance would predict. It remains the case that certain groups of pupils consistently fail to reach their potential while other groups of pupils consistently succeed, and that children from low-income families do not on average overcome the hurdle of lower initial attainment (West and Pennell 2003). So the odds, it would seem, are 'still stacked against schools in poorer areas' insofar that social class differential remains a powerful indicator of subsequent educational achievement (Gray 2001, p. 1).

The drive to raise standards in difficult or challenging contexts has also become a central and urgent issue in education policy in other countries. In the USA, this urgency has been underscored by the federal No Child Left Behind Act of 2001, which mandates an aggressive system of corrective measures for schools receiving federal assistance if they fail to meet progress goals. This policy and its relentless drive for system-wide improvement through increased accountability has a particular *déjà vu* quality, when comparing it to recent attempts in England to address the complex equation of disadvantage and underperformance. The 'school improvement' measures associated with No Child Left Behind of labelling, targeting and reconstitution (sometimes with private sector involvement) are no different from the penalties imposed upon under-performing schools in England. Both approaches are characterized by a high degree of accountability accompanied by myopia towards the wider social and economic problems that envelop the majority but not all of these schools.

Explanations for the poor performance of schools in disadvantaged areas are highly contested but the predominant message in the current policy drive is that the problem is internal to schools. If one accepts this position then it follows that the key to fixing the problem resides in getting staff within these schools to improve their practice, without looking too deeply or seriously at the contextual factors and influences affecting them or the schools in which they work. Consequently, compensatory measures coupled with increasing accountability have been a particular feature of New Labour's drive to improve the performance of schools in areas of acute disadvantage. This is seen most clearly in the Schools Facing Challenging Circumstances initiative, launched in 2001, which incorporated both additional funding and inspection visits as a means of improving schools in contexts of disadvantage.

The Schools Facing Challenging Circumstances initiative was a major part of the Standards and Effectiveness Unit's efforts to raise educational standards in schools in the most challenging contexts. The initiative aimed to provide targeted support for schools that fell below the 'floor targets' of A*–C at GCSE, which at that time was 25 per cent. The exact number of secondary schools in this category was approximately 600 and inevitably within this broad grouping the range of performance varied considerably. This group of schools contained the lowest performing schools in England and a disproportionate number of schools in special measures. Socio-economic disadvantage within this group of schools was high, with 36 per cent of pupils being registered for free school meals compared with a national average of 19 per cent (Reynolds *et al* 2001). Despite a recognition of the importance of context on performance through the categorization of 'challenging circumstances', it was generally felt that these schools could 'turn themselves around' and that the problem within the schools remained predominantly one of poor practice. The high profile of certain schools in difficult contexts who had 'turned themselves around' served only to reinforce the view that context was a barrier that could be overcome. It was considered possible for schools in 'challenging circumstances' to overcome acute advantage simply through their own efforts. But what exactly is meant by challenging circumstances?

The extent of the challenge

It is clear that schools located in disadvantaged areas suffer a myriad of socio-economic problems, such as high levels of unemployment, physical and mental health issues, migration of the best qualified young people and, not least, low educational achievement. In addition these schools are often in recipient of higher than average numbers of pupils with diverse ethnic backgrounds and low literacy levels on entry. In many cases, schools facing challenging circumstances (SfCC) may take a high proportion of refugee children or pupils that have been excluded from other schools. Not only does this make the student population inherently transient but it presents teachers with the daily task of teaching pupils whom they have not taught before. Inevitably this places great demands on teachers and often leaves the school in a position of having difficulty with teacher recruitment and retention.

It is clear that the 'challenging circumstances' descriptor is one that covers a wide range of possibilities and is not just concerned with material deprivation or poverty. It refers to the multiplicity of economic and social challenges that face certain schools and which, in certain combinations, lead to schools being in exceptionally challenging circumstances. These powerful, interlocking variables render the teaching and learning processes, accepted and expected in schools in more favourable circumstances, more difficult. As Power *et al* (2003) conclude in their study: '[educational] outcomes in deprived areas are worse than those in non-deprived areas, whether they are measured in terms of qualification, attendance, exclusions or "staying on" rates. Inner-city areas in particular feature as having low outcomes' (p. 26). They also point to the need to reduce the 'compositional effects that appear to result from high concentrations of disadvantaged students' (p. 65). What is being described here is a paucity of 'cultural and social capital' that makes it significantly more difficult for schools in challenging circumstances to improve.

It is clear that income, social class, ethnicity and gender all impact upon pupils' motivation levels and their predisposition to learning and educational achievement. In combination, these factors make the prospect of curriculum coverage and effective teaching and learning more difficult to achieve. There also appear to be a number of common external compounding factors that make the extent of the challenge facing these schools much worse. For example, the geographical isolation of rural schools, selective local educational systems, weak support from the LEA, low levels of formal qualifications in local adult population and poor employment opportunities make the prospect of long-term sustained improvement desirable rather than achievable.

The social capital that young people are equipped with and bring to school also differs enormously. The term 'cultural and social capital' derives from the work of Bourdieu (1987), who highlights the way that practices are infused (unequally) with social legitimation so that not all cultural practices are viewed as having equal value. Both 'cultural and social capital' are primarily concerned with the way in which social position is transformed into social advantage. Lamont and Lareau (1988, p156) define cultural capital as 'widely shared high status cultural signals used for social and cultural exclusion'. Implicit in this definition is the notion of inherent disadvantage perpetuated by a class system. Similarly, social capital refers to the social networks and relationships that advantage certain groupings over others. These social networks provide advantages in a highly differentiated social space and maintain deep divides within and between schools. In short, cultural capital and social capital are concerned with sustaining power relations and patterns of social and cultural domination. They provide middle-class families with invisible benefits not available to working-class and poor families.

Social capital is described by the OECD as the pattern and intensity of networks among people, the support they receive from those networks and the sense of well-being and empowerment that derive from shared values and trust in one's own environment. The idea of social capital is captured in three ways. The first of these concerns levels of trust insofar that individuals trust their neighbours, and whether their neighbourhood poses a threat. The second is social membership, which is measured by the number of organizations, clubs and social groups individuals belong to. The third concerns networks, as both informal and formal networks are central to the notion of social capital. These networks are defined as the personal relationships that are accumulated through interaction with various groupings.

It would appear that there are significant differences between these three interpretations across different income groups. While the more privileged enjoy wide networks and receive both financial and emotional support, many people in poorer neighbourhoods receive little if any additional support of this kind. Furthermore the research evidence would suggest that higher levels of social capital positively relate to health, employment and educational achievement. The reverse, it would seem, is also true. The OECD's PISA report draws attention to the fact that many of the characteristics of educational disadvantage are not amenable to educational policy and that educational achievement is only possible through closing the gap between the higher and lower income groups.

Leithwood and Steinbach (2002) suggest that there is a fourth type of social capital that is especially important in accounting for a pupil's ability to succeed in school. This consists of the habits and dispositions evident in family members' individual and collective responses to intellectual and other everyday problems. When such habits and dispositions are productive they constitute an enormous resource for children. Once these are acquired they serve to contribute to a child's sense of self-efficacy. There is much evidence to show that within middle-class families these dispositions are more visible and accessible. Conversely, families located in contexts of disadvantage are least able to generate and develop the forms of social capital that bring success. As Apple (2001, p. 73) explains:

> more affluent parents often have more flexible hours and can visit multiple schools. They have cars – often more than one – and can afford driving their children across town to attend a 'better school'. They can as well provide the hidden cultural resources such as camps and after school programmes (dance, music, computer classes etc.) that give their children an 'ease', a 'style' that seems 'natural' and acts as a set of cultural resources.

The converse of this position is that parents and families in poor and disadvantaged communities are less able to 'work the system', leaving more and more students in high poverty areas grouped together in the same school, thus reducing the social mix that has been shown to significantly influence a school's ability to improve its performance.

Despite extensive investment in external forms of intervention and support (e.g. Education Action Zones and Excellence in Cities) the Government's improvement targets for schools in disadvantaged communities or 'challenging contexts' have proved to be elusive. Part of the reason for this resides in the complexity and difficulty of the terrain as well as the predominant model of school improvement which is premised upon 'standards' as the main driving force of success. Evidence suggests that the 'marketization' of education has resulted in schools in disadvantaged contexts becoming *less* able to raise their performance (Ball 2003). In short, a combination of market individualism and control through constant and comparative assessment (i.e. league tables) has demoted certain schools to the lower echelons of performance, indefinitely. This is not to suggest that these schools cannot improve but simply to acknowledge that the task facing them is significantly harder and more daunting than that facing schools in more favourable circumstances.

Although SfCC share certain socio-economic characteristics and face
similar challenges, this is where the similarity ends. Unlike 'effective' or
'improving' schools, which research shows consistently share the same
characteristics, the inherent complexity of SfCCs means that they do
not readily demonstrate the same internal conditions or features. Recent
research has shown that schools at the bottom of the league tables of
performance are culturally very different, despite sharing similar sets
of characteristics or facing similar sets of external challenges (Harris
et al 2003). As Hargreaves (2004, p. 30) has recently argued, 'under-
performing schools are not all alike, the reasons for or nature of their
underperformance vary greatly'. This suggests that underperformance is
not a single phenomenon but a complex set of variables that interact in
different ways in different school contexts.

Schools located in areas of high socio-economic deprivation are more
likely to be populated with students typically categorized as 'disadvantaged' or 'at risk'. They generally face a greater risk of school failure in
comparison with their more affluent counterparts, and have significantly
lower levels of social and cultural capital. In addition, with disadvantage
comes diversity and the more severe the disadvantage the greater the
diversity within the student population (Harris and Chapman 2004).
The net result of these factors is that schools in disadvantaged contexts
have students who not only vary from one another but also vary from
the teacher in outlook, experience and other attributes directly linked
to success at school. In schools in disadvantaged contexts the social
stratification or class of students may be relatively homogeneous while
differences in race, ethnicity, religion and language vary enormously.
These variations expand disproportionately the lower down the socio-
economic scale schools go. Consequently, there are two inherent problems
facing these schools. As noted earlier, the first is the influence of social
mix upon a school's ability to generate the social and cultural capital
required for higher levels of performance (Thrupp 1999). The second is
the complexity of the teaching task presented by a less affluent student
population.

Students from disadvantaged backgrounds can challenge teachers'
conceptions of what to teach, what to expect of students and even how
to communicate with them (Knapp 2001). This is not to suggest a deficit
model of teaching in schools in difficult circumstances but simply to

acknowledge the extent of the task in securing levels of performance that schools in more affluent areas achieve with relative ease. Research has shown that in order to achieve and sustain improvement in such schools teachers must exceed what might be termed as 'normal efforts' (Maden 2001). They have to work much harder and be more committed than their peers in more favourable socio-economic circumstances. In addition, they have to maintain that effort in order to sustain improvement as success can be short-lived and fragile in difficult or challenging circumstances (Whitty 2002, p. 109).

It cannot be denied therefore that there is a strong negative correlation between most measures of social disadvantage and school achievement. However, this should not translate into a deterministic and pessimistic position of believing that there is little that can be done with schools in difficult or challenging contexts. While it is important to recognize the socio-cultural factors that sustain inequalities in educational achievement, cultural deficit models underestimate the potential of schools, teachers and students to 'buck the trend'. There is increasing evidence that schools facing difficult and challenging circumstances are able to add significant value to levels of student achievement and learning (Maden and Hillman 1993). There is also evidence to show that these schools can and do improve levels of student performance and achievement (Gray 2001; Reynolds, Harris and Clarke 2005).

Improving schools in challenging circumstances: the evidence

The basis for much of the theorizing about school improvement has tended not to focus on schools in high-poverty areas or schools with above average levels of deprivation. With some important exceptions (e.g. Barth *et al* 1999; Leithwood and Steinbach 2002; Borman *et al* 2000), the contemporary school improvement literature has not been overly concerned with schools facing difficult or challenging circumstances. Only relatively recently have researchers in England focused their expertise and attention upon leadership in 'failing' or 'ineffective' schools (e.g. Stoll and Myers 1998; Gray 2001; Harris and Chapman 2001). As Gray (2001, p33) concedes: 'We don't really know how much more difficult it is for schools serving disadvantaged communities to improve because much of the improvement research has ignored this dimension – that it is more difficult, however, seems unquestionable.'

In addition, relatively few of these studies have focused exclusively upon leadership practices or forms of leadership that have contributed directly to improving SfCC. The reason for this lack of attention resides predominantly in the inherent sensitivity and the complexity of the terrain. Schools that face multiple forms of disadvantage are least likely to be open to critical scrutiny or exposure because they are most often the schools where academic performance is below average. While social disadvantage may not be an excuse for poor achievement in academic terms, it certainly is a powerful factor and source of explanation.

Schools in deprived areas often have multiple problems, including lost public support, challenging pupils, high levels of staff turnover and frequently a poor physical environment, which can lead to them being less effective. Reynolds *et al* (2001) list the characteristics of less successful schools:

- unwillingness to accept evidence of failure;
- blaming others (e.g. parents) for failure);
- fear of change and outsiders;
- cliques and dysfunctional relationships between staff;
- goals that are not relevant or plausible;
- lack of academic focus;
- passive attitude towards recruitment and training;
- not data-rich;
- not outcomes oriented;
- improvement strategies adopted but not properly implemented;
- inconsistent teaching quality;
- low expectations;
- emphasis on supervision and routines;
- low levels of pupil–teacher interaction;
- lots of negative feedback from teachers;
- teachers perceived as uncaring by pupils.

Gray (2000) adds to this list 'slowly paced lessons and high truancy and delinquency', while in a study of Memphis schools Etheridge, Butler and Scipio (1994) found schools that were lacking in 'academic press' (i.e. the pursuit of the highest academic outcomes) had no home–school programmes, and no preparation for higher education in secondary schools. Gray's (2000) study of schools coming out of 'special measures' found that in order to improve, these schools needed first and foremost to accept the need to change, plus the need to involve parents and governors. Teachers often need a new 'exciting idea' to galvanize them, such as a new teaching strategy, coupled with large amounts of professional development.

Both (Reynolds *et al* 2004) and (Hopkins 2001) in their reviews of school improvement in SfCC agree that strong early intervention is a necessity, and that ineffective schools need strong external intervention and support (Hopkins and Reynolds 2001). Some authors posit that it is necessary to start with easy-to-change aspects, such as brightening up the physical environment of the school (Hopkins and Reynolds 2001). That the physical environment matters is borne out by a study conducted by Reynolds, Stringfield and Muijs (forthcoming) in which the ten components of the High Reliability study were correlated with changes in achievement (GCSE A*–C %) between 1994 and 2001. Well-maintained equipment was also one of the factors most highly correlated to outcomes. Maden and Hillman (1993) similarly found that schools that were improving in disadvantaged areas were characterized by improvements in their immediate environment.

In their large-scale study of effective schools in disadvantaged areas, Maden and Hillman (1993) found that most improvement efforts were started by the head, but that teachers needed to get involved early on to make the improvement work. In their interviews with 25 heads of effective inner city schools in New York, Seeley, Niemeyer and Greenspan (1990) found that heads reported that they had implemented many reforms simultaneously, without however expecting instantaneous change or results. Another New York study (Connell 1996) found that schools who had improved to the extent that they were no longer on the official list of failing schools had focused on academic achievement by implementing new teaching and learning strategies.

Major structural changes, such as creating mini-schools or introducing team teaching, can provide both a positive, galvanizing focus, and change attitudes to change in schools in difficulty (Piontek *et al* 1998). Sometimes staff changes may be needed both at management and at teacher level, in order to give the school a fresh start (Hopkins and Reynolds 2001).

Connell (1996) in his study of New York schools found that eight out of ten improving schools had made significant staff changes.

Despite concerted attempts to tackle this particular problem, there remains an urgent need to secure ways of raising student achievement in schools located in areas of higher than average socio-economic deprivation. Hopkins and Reynolds (2001, p. 461) highlight how a wide range of work has been undertaken with the chief aim of assisting schools in challenging circumstances to improve. Initially, they highlight that this work resulted in:

- The generation of a review that sought to locate the present state of school improvement so that work could be conceptually up to date (Hopkins and Reynolds 2001).
- The generation of literature reviews about the school development planning process (Hopkins and Reynolds 2001) and the implications of research in school effectiveness and school improvement for what schools could do to improve themselves (Reynolds *et al* 2001).
- A series of seminars and meetings for the heads and other senior managers in the schools, designed to both update them with knowledge about 'what might work' and also provide systems of mutual support that would help generate increased 'educational resilience' in practitioners exposed to multiple stresses.

As noted earlier, over the last three or four years a concerted effort has been made to raise the performance of SfCC through a combination of increased resources, various developmental programmes and targeted professional development opportunities. In addition, specific funding and alternative approaches to improvement have emerged, intended specifically to assist schools in difficult circumstances. Most recently, the London Challenge and the Leadership Incentive Grant have both targeted schools in areas of disadvantage or 'challenging circumstances'. Yet, explanations for the poor quality of schools in disadvantaged areas remain contested.

While the dominant view is that the problem is internal to the school, it is unequivocally the case that not all schools in poor areas offer a poor education. Recent research by Lupton (2004, p. 3) has shown that five out of six schools with high free school meals (FSM) numbers are not adjudged to need substantial improvement in the quality of education, climate, management or efficiency. This would suggest that a disadvantaged or deprived socio-economic context does not in itself determine school failure or indeed predispose a school towards underperformance. Instead, it is asserted that the explanation for the poor performance resides in the interface between external (contextual) factors and internal (teaching quality) factors. The effects of context on professional practice are often assumed but not exposed or examined as the real basis for underperformance. Instead, as Thrupp (1999) and others have rightly pointed out, both policy-makers and researchers have produced generic notions of 'good practice' based upon exemplary schools where good leadership and teaching appear to have overcome the problems of the disadvantaged context, rather than bringing out the effects of context upon practice. Recent research by Reynolds *et al* (2005) has started to explore the relationship between external and internal factors and the way different combinations impact upon a school's ability to improve. This research, which looked at ten improving schools in the former coalfield areas, concluded that in the majority of cases shifts in the external environment (e.g. new employment opportunities, new housing, specialist status) had positively affected the school's ability to raise attainment far more than any internal changes (e.g. new buildings, new staff, new resources). Consequently, the power of context in the school improvement equation must not be underestimated, and for schools in exceptionally challenging circumstances this has a much greater impact.

The next chapter provides an overview of a government-funded programme of intervention specifically aimed at schools in the exceptionally challenging contexts. The OCTET project remains one of the few examples of an attempt to generate and develop an innovative improvement programme in conjunction with a small group of schools. As noted earlier, most school improvement interventions (e.g. High Reliability, Success for All, Accelerated Schools) tend to have a clear programme specification and rely on faithful implementation to achieve the results. As such they are ill-equipped to experiment, re-design or to reframe their approach in response to school need. In the case of the OCTET project the opportunity to evolve and develop a programme provided a unique opportunity to match programme design to contextual demands and constraints. This is not to suggest that the OCTET programme was content or structure free, as this was not the case, but rather to acknowledge that the high degree of flexibility and responsiveness of the programme to the contexts and needs of the eight schools was innovative and groundbreaking.

References

Apple, M. (1982) *Cultural and Economic Reproduction in Education*. London: Routledge & Kegan Paul.

Apple, M. (2001) *Educating the Right Way*. London: Falmer Press.

Ball, S. (2003) *Class Strategies and the Education Market: The Middle Classes and Social Advantage*. London: Routledge/Falmer.

Barth, P., Haycock, K., Jackson, H., Mora, K., Ruiz, P., Robinson, S. and Wilkins, A. (1999) *Dispelling the Myth. High Poverty Schools Exceeding Expectations*. Washington: The Education Trust.

Bordieu, P. (1987) 'Forms of capital', in Richardson, J. G. (ed.) *Handbook of Theory and Research for Sociology of Education*, 241–58. New York: Oxford.

Borman, G. D., Rachuba, L., Datnow, A., Alberg, M., Maciver, M. and Stringfield, S. (2000) *Four Models of School Improvement. Successes and Challenges in Reforming Low-Performing, High Poverty Title 1 Schools*. Baltimore: Johns Hopkins University, Center for Research into the Education of Students Placed At Risk.

Connell, N. (1996) *Getting off the List: School Improvement in New York City*. New York: New York City Educational Priorities Panel.

DfEE (1997) *Excellence in Schools*. London: HMSO.

Etheridge, G. W., Butler, E. D. and Scipio, J. E. April 4–9, 1994) *Design of a Learning Community for Urban Learners: The Memphis Plan*. Paper presented at the Annual Meeting of the American Educational Research Association, New Orleans.

Gray, J. (2000) *Causing Concern but Improving: A Review of Schools' Experiences*. London: Department for Education and Skills.

Gray, J. (2001). 'Introduction', in *Success Against the Odds: Five Years On*. London: Routledge.

Gray, J. (2004) 'Frames of reference and traditions of interpretation: Some issues in the identification of "under-achieving" schools.' *British Journal of Educational Studies*, Vol. 52 No. 3, 293–309.

Hargreaves, A. (2004) 'Distinction and disgust: The emotional politics of school failure.' *International Journal of Leadership in Education Theory and Practice*, 27–43.

Harris, A., and Chapman, C. (2001) *Leadership in Schools Facing Challenging Circumstances*. London: Department for Education and Skills.

Harris, A. and Chapman, C. (2004) 'Towards differentiated improvement for schools in challenging circumstances.' *British Journal of Educational Studies,* Vol. 52, No. 4, 27–36.

Harris A., Muijs, D., Chapman, C., Stoll, L. and Russ, J. (2003) *Raising Attainment in Former Coalfield Areas.* Sheffield: Department for Education and Skills.

Henderson, R. (1975) *Poverty in Australia.* Canberra: AGPS.

Hopkins, D. (2001) *School Improvement for Real.* London: Routledge.

Hopkins, D. and Reynolds, D. (2001). 'The past, present and future of school improvement: towards the Third Age.' *British Educational Research Journal,* Vol. 27, No. 4, 459–75.

Knapp, M. S. (2001) 'Policy, poverty and capable teaching', in Biddle, B. (ed.) *Social Class, Poverty and Education.* London: Routledge.

Lamont, M. and Lareau, A. (1988) 'Cultural capital: Allusions, gaps and glissandos.' *Sociological Theory,* 6, 153–68.

Leithwood, K. and Steinbach, R. (2002) 'Successful leadership for especially challenging schools.' *Journal of Leadership in Education,* 79(2), 73–82.

Lupton, R. (2004) *Schools in disadvantaged areas: Recognising context and raising performance.* CASE paper 76, London: Centre for Analysis of Social Exclusion, London School of Economics and Political Science.

Maden, M. (ed.) (2001) *Success Against the Odds: Five Years On.* London: Routledge.

Maden, M. and Hillman, J. (eds) (1993) *Success Against the Odds: Effective Schools in Disadvantage Areas.* London: Routledge.

National Commission of Education (NCE) (1996) *Success Against the Odds: Effective Schooling in Disadvantaged Areas.* London: Routledge.

Ofsted (2003) *Section 10 Evidence for Deprived Urban Schools.* London: Ofsted.

Piontek, M. E., Dwyer, M. C., Seager, A. and Orsburn, C. (1998) *Capacity for Reform: Lessons from High Poverty Urban Elementary Schools.* Portsmouth, NH: RMC Research Corporation.

Power, S., Warren, S., Gillbourn, D., Clark, A., Thomas, S. and Kelly, C. (2003) *Education in Deprived Areas. Outcomes, Inputs and Processes.* London: Institute of Education, University of London.

Rainwater, L. and Smeeding, T. (2003) *Poor Kids in a Rich Country. America's Children in Comparative Perspective.* New York: Russell Sage Foundation.

Reynolds, D. (1986) *School Effectiveness.* London: Falmer Press.

Reynolds, D., Harris, A. and Clarke, C. (2005) 'Challenging the challenged: Improving schools in difficulty.' *International Journal of School Effectiveness and School improvement* (forthcoming).

Reynolds, D., Hopkins, D., Potter, D. and Chapman, C. (2001) *School Improvement for Schools Facing Challenging Circumstances: A Review of Research and Practice.* London: Department for Education and Skills.

Reynolds, D., Stringfield, S. and Muijs, D. (forthcoming). *Results from the High Reliability Schools Project.* Unpublished manuscript.

Rutter, M., Mortimore, P. and Maugham, B. (1979) *Fifteen Thousand Hours. Secondary Schools and their Effects.* Boston: Harvard University Press.

Seeley, D. S., Niemeyer, J. S. and Greenspan, R. (1990) *Principals Speak: Improving Inner-City Elementary Schools. Report on Interviews with 25 New York City Principals.* New York: City University of New York.

Smith, T. and Noble, M. (1995) *Education Divides: Poverty and Schooling in the 1990s.* London: Child Poverty Action Group.

Stoll, L. and Myers, K. (1998) *No Quick Fixes. Perspectives on Schools in Difficulty.* London: Falmer Press.

Teese, R., and Polesal, J. (eds) (2003) *Undemocratic schooling. Equity and Quality in Mass Secondary Education in Australia.* Sydney: Allen & Unwin.

Thrupp, M. (1999) *Schools Making a Difference: Let's Be Realistic! School Mix, School Effectiveness and the Social Limits of Reform.* Ballmoor: Open University Press.

West, A. and Pennell, H. (2003) *Underachievement in Schools.* London: Falmer Press.

Whitty, G. (2002) 'Education, social class and social exclusion.' *Education & Social Justice,* 1(1), 2–8.

2 The OCTET Project

Introduction

In November 2000 government ministers approved the development of a pilot project with a small group of well-managed secondary schools, which faced exceptionally challenging circumstances. It was generally recognized by the government that there was a real need to improve the quality of education for children with low prior attainment, poor motivation and low self-esteem, and move them towards achieving their potential. In the following year a research and development project was commissioned by the DfES with the prime purpose of working with a group of eight schools located in the greatest 'category' of challenge in the English education system, i.e. 'schools facing exceptionally challenging circumstances' (SfECC). Put simply, these schools were located in communities which continue to face some of the most difficult economic and social challenges. All faced the issues of poverty, poor housing, poor social welfare, and in some cases difficult inter-cultural relations. The aim of the project was to work with eight secondary schools over a two- to three-year timescale to generate an intensive programme of intervention and improvement that could potentially be replicated in other schools facing 'extreme challenges'. This project became known as the 'OCTET project' and a specifically tailored school improvement for the eight schools was designed.

The programme design was consistent with what Hopkins and Reynolds (2001) have termed 'third wave' school improvement. Hopkins and Reynolds (2001, p. 3) outline these three phases of school improvement as follows:

- The first phase was epitomized by the OECD's International School Improvement Project (ISIP), but unfortunately many of the initiatives associated with this first phase of school improvement were 'free floating', rather than representing a systematic, programmatic and coherent approach to school change. There was correspondingly, in this phase, an emphasis upon organizational change, school self-evaluation and the 'ownership of change' by individual schools and teachers, but these initiatives were loosely connected to student learning outcomes, both conceptually and practically, were variable and fragmented in conception and application, and consequently in the eyes of most school improvers the practices struggled to impact upon classroom practice (Hopkins 2001; Reynolds 1998).

- The second phase of development began in the early 1990s and resulted from the interaction between the school improvement and the school effectiveness communities. In these years the school improvement tradition was beginning to provide schools with guidelines and strategies for implementation that were sufficiently powerful to begin to take educational change into classrooms. Approaches to staff development based upon partnership teaching (Joyce and Showers 1995), and designs for development planning that focused upon learning outcomes and which linked together organizational and classroom change within a medium-term time frame, are but two examples of the school improvement contribution. Fullan (1991) provides a useful survey of the first two ages of this school improvement enterprise.

- The third phase of school improvement developed from the somewhat uncomfortable evidence that the wide range of national educational reforms produced in various countries, as well as the contributions of the school improvement communities of many countries, may not have been particularly successful. Despite the dramatic increase in education reform efforts in most countries, their impact upon overall levels of student achievement are widely seen as not having been as successful as anticipated. Although there may have been pockets of relatively short-lived success in certain countries, such as the National Literacy and Numeracy strategies in England (Fullan 2001), and individual programmes which appear to be effective over time, such as *Success for All* (Slavin 1996), the evidence from major programmes such as 'New American Schools' is the limitations of 'off the shelf' improvement or 'whole school designs' in securing long-term and widespread system and school improvement.

Hopkins and Reynolds (2001) note there are of course variations between these various programmes that make any global assessment difficult. Nevertheless, if one were to compare these examples of third wave school improvement as a group, Hopkins and Reynolds (2001, p. 464) suggest, it is clear that:

- There has been an enhanced focus upon the importance of pupil outcomes. Instead of the earlier emphasis upon changing the processes of schools, the focus is now upon seeing if these changes are powerful enough to affect pupil outcomes.
- The learning level and the instructional behaviours of teachers have been increasingly targeted for explicit attention, rather than the school level.
- There has been the creation of an infrastructure to enable the knowledge base, both 'best practice' and research findings, to be utilized. This has involved an internal focus on collaborative patterns of staff development that enable teachers to enquire into practice, and external strategies for dissemination and networking.
- There has been an increasing consciousness of the importance of 'capacity building'. This includes not only staff development, but also medium-term strategic planning and change strategies that utilize 'pressure and support', as well as the intelligent use of external support agencies.
- There has been an adoption of a 'mixed' methodological orientation, in which bodies of quantitative data plus qualitative data are used to measure quality, and variation in that quality. This includes an audit of existing classroom and school processes and outcomes, and comparison with desired end states, in particular the educational experiences of different pupil groups.
- There has been an increased emphasis upon the importance of ensuring reliability or 'fidelity' in programme implementation across all organizational members within schools, in marked contrast with the past when improvement programmes did not have to be organizationally 'tight'.
- There has been an appreciation of the importance of cultural change in order to embed and sustain school improvement. There has been a focus on a careful balance between 'vision building' and the adapting of structures to support those aspirations.
- There has been also an increased concern to ensure that the improvement programmes relate to, and impact upon, practitioners and practices through using increasingly sophisticated training, coaching and development programmes.

These 'third wave' practices and philosophies of school improvement provided the theoretical, conceptual and practical framework for the programme design, particularly for the staff development component of the OCTET project. A number of key principles were taken from the research base and 'third wave' school improvement efforts that shaped the subsequent staff development provision. These principles were fourfold:

- to establish a way of working conducive to experimentation;
- to explore innovative approaches to teaching and learning;
- to develop a strong network of schools;
- to explore the potential of inter-school support i.e. the power of eight.

In terms of the programme design there were some 'tight' and 'loose' components. The tight components or non-negotiable elements were as follows:

- a focus on utilizing data for informing teaching and learning;
- attention to the processes of teaching and learning;
- attention to the affective/emotional domain;
- a requirement for inter-school sharing.

The loose or less prescriptive elements of the staff development programme were the ability of schools to shape and influence the content of the programme and to focus attention on the developmental issues that were important to their school in their context.

The schools

Eight schools were chosen to be part of the pilot project on the grounds of being in exceptionally disadvantaged communities, and having low attainment at Key Stage 4 but also being well led. Even in these well-led and well-managed schools, it was clear that the proportion of pupils attaining good academic results remained well below floor target level. For instance, in 2000 across the eight project schools 11% of pupils achieved five A*–C grades at GCSE, and the target at that time was one of 20% by 2004. Consequently, the subsequent research and development project aimed to test new improvement practices, and to gauge which proved most effective. The prime objective was to develop a new school improvement programme for use with a wider group of schools facing difficult circumstances.

There was a long list of between 20 and 30 schools which were initially considered. In March 2001 the DfES agreed the participation of eight schools,[3] and the direction of the project, which was to develop and test a range of interventions to raise attainment and improve the life chances of pupils. Among these eight schools attainment at Key Stage 4 varied year from year from 1% to 25%. The eight schools provided a geographical spread and while sharing many characteristics, the schools were very different from each other. They ranged in size from just over 400 to almost 1,200 students and there was a sharp divide between those schools which were mono-ethnic (Campion, Havelock, Pennywell, The Channel, The Ridings) and those who were multi-ethnic (St Albans, Phoenix, Whitefield). As the project began, all eight schools were experiencing common challenges. These challenges can be summarized as follows:

- high staff and student mobility;
- negative perceptions of the community: the image of the school;
- pressure from outside: LEA, HMI Ofsted;
- internal and external turbulence;
- competition from local schools;
- an intake disproportionably high in students with extra learning needs including EAL, literacy levels and special educational needs.

An analysis of the transfer of pupils at Key Stage 2 showed how competition from more popular schools negatively affected the OCTET schools' intake. The existence of grammar schools and selective schools, in some areas, has had a negative impact upon the school intake and for some schools this is exacerbated by the sheer numbers of primary feeder schools, ranging between 30 and 70 schools. Within the OCTET schools there is a student body which contains a disproportionably high number of students with special learning needs: 42.2 per cent in Whitefields and 64.7 per cent in St Albans. All OCTET schools have abnormally high levels of students in the special educational needs category in comparison

---

3 Schools committed to the project are: Campion High School, Liverpool; Havelock School, Grimsby; Pennywell School, Sunderland; Phoenix High School, Hammersmith & Fulham, London; St Albans CE School, Birmingham; The Channel School, Folkestone; The Ridings School, Halifax; and Whitefield School, Barnet.

with other neighbouring secondary schools. While the impact of social mix on school performance is well known, it is clear that in the case of the OCTET schools this was particularly acute and problematic.

In addition, all the OCTET schools had at some time suffered from acute staff recruitment and retention problems. Staff shortages remain particularly high at all schools, but for the Phoenix School the problem continues to be severe. At any one time the crisis can be as high as 30 per cent understaffing and the daily challenge is one of finding adequate supply teachers to fill the gaps. Similarly, high and persistent levels of student mobility continue to be a problem at a number of the schools. This high turnover of students coupled with the turnover of staff means a continuously shifting and unpredictable teaching and learning terrain which is very different from the average secondary school.

Along with this constantly shifting pattern of staffing and students within each school is the external turbulence and pressure that can be caused by negative media coverage. The Ridings, and most recently St Albans, offer examples of this phenomenon and its detrimental effects. In November 1996 The Ridings suffered heavily from adverse publicity and became labelled as the 'worse school in England'. As a result of media attention and unfounded allegations, the Phoenix School continues to attract negative press on occasions. Consequently, the negative perception of the schools within the community is difficult to shift and to change despite tangible and demonstrable improvements in performance.

Recent influential and powerful work by Lupton (2004) has highlighted that despite having common characteristics such as the indicators of disadvantage, schools in high-poverty areas also are distinctive in other aspects that they share. Her work notes that the disadvantaged contexts of the schools are influential in terms of generating numerous small process effects that together contribute to a school environment that is characteristically different from those schools in more advantaged settings. These effects are outlined under five headings: additional learning needs; material poverty; the emotional climate and disturbed behaviour; reluctant poverty; and the unpredictable school. Each of these five areas outlined by Lupton (2004) will briefly be considered in relation to the OCTET group of schools.

It is clear that the OCTET schools have a wide range of abilities and very low levels of prior attainment. In particular, the extreme learning needs of the lowest attaining pupils are very different from those experienced by schools in more favourable circumstances. These additional learning needs across all the schools prove difficult to meet because of the extra demands upon staff. Even with learning support provision, it is evident that on a daily basis most of these schools struggle to meet the weight of learning demands. As a result, in many schools teaching approaches are adapted and carefully adjusted to address learning styles or the prior attainment of pupils. However, research suggests that teaching for many lower ability pupils in SfCC tends to be for control and containment and as a result is insufficiently challenging.

A second issue raised by Lupton's (2004) work and reflected in the OCTET schools is one of material poverty. None of the schools could expect financial contributions from parents and pupils for equipment or materials. Few pupils in any of the OCTET schools could be assumed to have any learning resources at home such as books or a computer and in addition, very few had access to external resources such as libraries. On a daily basis also the issue of resources for learning within schools presented a problem. Pupils tend not come to lessons with even the most basic equipment such as a pen, which means a great deal of lesson time is spent handing out and retrieving pens, pencils and other equipment.

The third and potentially most distinctive aspect of schools like those within the OCTET schools is the fact that they all have a charged emotional environment. The heads themselves recognize that there are pupils in their schools who are anxious, traumatized, abused and unhappy. This proportion is significantly higher than in schools with more affluent contexts and pupil populations. Inevitably, these emotional difficulties translate themselves into behavioural problems and impact upon other pupils and staff in the school. It appears that most of the behavioural issues that teachers face in their classroom are bound up with emotional problems and difficulties located outside the school itself. Low attendance is also a problem across all the OCTET schools and there are high proportions of absences from persistent non-attendees. This suggests that these schools are dealing with a higher than average number of exceptionally disaffected pupils even if the vast majority of pupils attend for most of the time. This factor coupled with high pupil mobility makes the pupil population a hugely variable factor which is difficult to manage on a day-to-day basis.

It is Lupton's (2004) contention that when you add up all these distinctive features or characteristics of schools in extreme poverty you have an unpredictable and sometimes volatile working environment. At any time incidents may erupt that can destabilise and erode the possibility of any teaching or learning. Unplanned events impact dramatically on senior managers who are constantly managing the tension inherent in a school in exceptionally challenging circumstances. As a result strategic issues and developmental work can be disrupted and paperwork and planning are simply not possible in school hours. Overall, schools in exceptionally challenging circumstances, such as those schools in the OCTET project, have multiple problems that, at times, can render them impotent against contextual forces. However, it is also clear that the dedication, persistence and high professional standards of the staff in the school can offset some of the more negative influences that amalgamate on a daily basis.

The OCTET project

The Schools facing Exceptionally Challenging Circumstances Project (SfECC), which subsequently became known as the OCTET project, was announced in the Green Paper *Schools: Building on Success*. Each of the eight schools met the following criteria: 15 per cent or fewer of their pupils achieving five A*–C GCSE grades in 1999 and 2000; 40 per cent or more eligible to free school meals; 39 per cent or more with special educational needs; and assessed as having good or better management at their most recent Ofsted assessment. Recurrent funding in the financial year 2001–02 was allocated at £150,000 per school and was available to the schools from September 2001. Funding at this level continued for a further two years directly linked to the project's progress and strategies being trialled.

While it was acknowledged that the challenges facing the OCTET schools were substantial, they were all considered to be 'ready' to enter the project. Many of the schools already had a large number of initiatives (internal and external) underway and therefore in some cases OCTET supplemented existing initiatives while in others it replaced them. At the start of the project the eight schools were judged to be focusing on a range of strategies to meet the challenges they faced. These strategies included:

- efforts to stabilize staffing and build on the core of committed staff;
- focus on the consistency of basic teaching and learning practices;
- some key appointments, particularly at middle and senior management level;
- strong management systems;
- emphasis on improving ethos and image;
- enhancement of a culture of care and respect;
- concentration on behaviour and attendance.

Clearly within each of the schools the range and combinations of strategies varied but there was a high level of commitment to improvement and raising student performance. The OCTET project was voluntary but carried a large amount of resource and the opportunity to engage in experimentation and innovation. It was this last aspect that chiefly attracted all eight schools to agree to take part in the programme.

Each school was expected to work with other organizations in its community to integrate activities, where appropriate, with existing local programmes for community regeneration. The DfES was committed to supporting each school to maintain a system of individual pupil records to allow tracking of pupils' progress and to measure the impact of the different inputs. The project also linked with Excellence in Cities, Education Action Zones and Excellence Clusters, as well as with programmes which provide support to individual schools with particular challenges, such as Schools Facing Challenging Circumstances (around 600 schools) and Fresh Start. The project also linked with the Key Stage 3 strategy and CPD strategy, both of which were concerned with the professional development of teachers, as well as with the social inclusion agenda and its focus on pupil behaviour and discipline and under achievement.

At the outset, the OCTET project aimed to improve academic performance, and so benefit the life chances of individuals and reduce the level of dependency on the state and the likelihood of criminal involvement. This outcome was in line with the first of the DfES's central objectives, 'Ensuring that all young people reach 16 with the skills, attitudes, and personal qualities that will give them a secure foundation for lifelong learning, work and citizenship in a rapidly changing world.' The principle objectives of the SfECC programme were as follows:

- To test successful existing school improvement programmes and to work together to identify and develop new ones.
- To achieve the floor target – that all schools should achieve 20% five GCSEs at grades A*–C by 2004, and 25% by 2006.
- To develop each school as 'a professional learning community', where teachers not only plan together, but also observe each other and gather formative data on the impact the various strategies are having on student learning. It was agreed that OFSTED would monitor progress in the pilot schools and comment on the effectiveness of the strategies that are in place particularly as they impact on teaching and learning.
- To play a key role in generating new approaches to school improvement, particularly for schools in difficult contexts.

In summary, OCTET was not designed to be 'another initiative'. Rather it was intended to complement existing initiatives and to contribute to the development of a coherent improvement strategy. Where appropriate, this involved working closely with partners through the Local Strategic Partnership (LSP) and the wider community, including ethnic minorities, taking into account the priorities set by the LSP in its community strategy and local neighbourhood renewal strategy.

The OCTET improvement strategies that were tested by the schools included:

- Effective use of adults other than teachers to: provide counselling/mentoring for pupils; provide support for behaviour management; support the delivery of curriculum packages; and support classroom teaching.
- More time for teachers to prepare and assess work and to undertake curriculum planning with staff from other schools.
- More flexible approaches to pupil grouping and the option of smaller classes.
- The effective use of individual learning packages linked to regular formalized target-setting sessions.
- Assessing the quality of computer-aided learning packages and 'curriculum recovery' packs for pupils working below National Curriculum expectations.

- Use of ICT to enhance curriculum delivery and overcome school limitations in specialist subjects.
- Greater flexibility in the curriculum to focus on the basics throughout and provide options for work-based learning.
- Impact of bonuses and other inducements to recruit and retain staff of high quality.
- A commissioned programme of staff development.

The main driver behind the project was the development of staff in the OCTET schools. The majority of funding was used on various forms of teacher development and to buy teaching resources. The major training programmes provided by the OCTET project were for middle managers, for members of the school improvement group (SIG), for teachers using the reading programme RML, and ICT training in the use of interactive whiteboards. Bespoke training was also offered to the senior management team in some schools.

The middle management training involved three to five teachers from each of the schools who participated in two training opportunities. The training was project focused and required teachers to apply the principles learned back in their own school context. The RML reading programme comprised of two components, RML1 and RML2, with a phonics based programme for Key Stage 2 and 3 pupils. It was aimed at pupils who found it difficult to understand or decode text. The programme was tightly prescribed and taught in the schools for one hour a day up to four times a week. The training for RML took place over two days and was supplemented with visits to schools and additional training. The inter-active whiteboard training was provided for technicians and support staff in all schools prior to a one-day event at Phoenix School in November 2002. The focus was on Maths, Science, English and foreign languages. The training was of a practical nature allowing participants to focus upon their own subject. The training in the use of CAT data took place in 2002 in two regional groupings and looked at the use of software to analyse CAT data.

The major strand of work in teacher development was the SIG training. Each school was asked to identify a group of between six and eight teachers to form a SIG which was intended to be the catalyst for change and development within the school. A specially commissioned programme of staff development was secured to offer training to the SIGs. This training was required to have the following features: good presentation/description of learning theories; skills and practical strategies; taught classroom organization linked to theories of learning; preferred learning styles explained and effects on teaching strategies explored; modelling/demonstration (for real or via video); opportunity to practise in classrooms with feedback on performance; ongoing coaching/mentoring post training; takeaways and support materials; and line managers briefed on expectations post training

This programme was awarded to a group of researchers and trainers who worked with the SIGs from each of the eight schools for two years (Reynolds, Clarke and Harris 2004). Early discussions with the heads identified that this staff development programme was viewed by the schools as a means of experimenting with established knowledge bases concerning teaching and learning. It was seen as a way of enhancing school capacity building by introducing new pedagogical approaches which challenged students and enthused and engaged staff. Initial face-to-face planning only allowed time for three meetings with heads: after each meeting they returned to their schools and consulted with their staff. This channel of communication between the heads, their colleagues in school and the SIG training team generated a number of shared issues and principles, as well as representing an emergent collaborative way of working.

It was agreed that both schools and programme team wanted to:

- establish a way of working that was conducive to experimentation;
- explore and improvise with innovative approaches to teaching and in the support of learning;
- deepen the competence of the school-based teams through very deliberate strategies which would encourage collegial practice;
- explore ways of taking advantage of the inter-school dimension of the programme by encouraging the reporting of findings and sharing of school-based experiences with colleagues from other school sites involved in the programme.

It was also agreed that the SIG development programme would comprise certain components. As noted earlier, the 'tight' components were a focus on data to highlight areas for change, attention to the instructional processes, attention to the emotional or affective domain and lastly a requirement of inter-school sharing i.e. the power of eight. The staff development programme was designed in a way that allowed for choice and differentiation across different school sites. The programme did not prescribe the ways of working adopted by the school improvement groups or how the SIG chose to disseminate and activate key developments in teaching and learning within their own school context. The SIGs operated with a great deal of autonomy and were seen by the programme team as the main catalysts for change and development.

The main aim of the staff development programme was to move the SIGs from initial dependency to independency and eventually interdependency. The staff development programme encompassed two central dimensions: a theory of instruction based upon certain bodies of knowledge about effective teaching and models of teaching; and a theory of practice based upon the theory of action learning and action research principles. Throughout the life of the project, the programme combined a theory of instruction and a theory of practice, ensuring that there was a clear relationship between the training and the subsequent action on return to the school.

Early stages of the project

It was clear in the early stages that it was important that the SfECC project was not seen in a deficit way and that the schools involved felt that it was an opportunity to be engaged in highly selective programme of support. The sensitivities of the terrain could not be underestimated and therefore a great deal of time was spent in the initial phases talking to and negotiating with the eight heads. This open dialogue continued throughout the project. Also at a fairly early stage in the project it became obvious that the human resource required some radical re-thinking. The project schools considered some innovative restructuring to address the variable staffing 'conditions' that they faced. Some of the strategies tested by the schools included:

- An audit of the impact of the work of Adults Other than Teachers, leading to more effective deployment.

- Broader use of Adults Other than Teachers to provide counselling/ mentoring for pupils; support for behaviour management; the delivery of curriculum packages; and support for classroom teaching, administration and technical provision.
- Setting this deployment within a process of credit-worthy training and a new career structure.
- Creating more time for teachers to prepare and assess work and to undertake curriculum planning with staff from other schools through adjustments to the timetable and the appointment of 'permanent supply' staff.
- More flexible approaches to pupil grouping and the option of smaller classes.

Also the extra funding available to the project schools meant that they could consider:

- The balance between leadership group, teaching and support staff.
- The arrangement of management roles with responsibility for pupils and the priority awarded to the management and support of staff.
- The extent of the contribution of support staff to teaching, adminis-tration and management work and for the first time allowing some means of assessing their impact on school improvement.
- Use of new grades and job titles e.g. Assistant Heads, Learning Managers, Deputy Head – School Improvement, Director for Teaching and Learning.
- Recruitment and retention, lock-ins and honoraria.
- The use of 'locum' heads of department and the internal deployment of Advanced Skills Teachers.
- The use of temporary and fixed-term contracts, including the support and induction of staff trained overseas.
- The training and advice necessary to enhance the governing body role in terms of staffing, management and human resources including appointments.

The project schools were also encouraged to think creatively about their recent and past practice with regard to:-

- Policy and pay relatives across the school. Historical structures were found not always suitable to meet current needs.

- Pay discretions and rewards for enhanced performance.
- The use of pay and benefits to achieve a stable recruitment and retention position, including planning for succession and trailing new approaches to overcome issues of recruitment.
- The use of Adults Other than Teachers and Para-Professionals across a broad range of activities.

As with most other schools, the project schools were generally very busy undertaking CPD activity. The main issues faced by most of the OCTET schools seem to be focused on post-training implementation and in-school support for innovation. Schools were therefore asked to consider:

- How are the development needs of all staff identified?
- How are funds and release time prioritized for maximum benefit and minimum disruption?
- How could they improve the selection and availability of suitable and targeted training?
- How could they manage implementation and change in practice resulting from training using new models of post-training support?
- How could they assess the impact on performance and ensure facilitative structural changes are made to support innovation?

Schools within the project took part in a significant training programme for their middle managers. Once trained in school improvement activities they were also required to act as mentors to another departmental head on returning to school. They were expected to generate an 11-week Raising Attainment Plan within their colleague's department as well as within their own. All project schools identified a SIG made up of credible, influential colleagues who have been given time to support innovation and provide school-based activity, including peer observation, further technical training and support. Their main brief was to ensure good creative ideas and new approaches were fostered and carried through, and that the process of introducing change in some of our most challenging classrooms was supported.

Success of SfECC

In 2005 the OCTET schools had improved the A–C scores significantly.[4] How much these improvements can be claimed by the OCTET project is difficult to ascertain as the schools were involved in many other initiatives and developments. The Cambridge evaluation of the project suggested that the schools felt that certain aspects of OCTET had contributed to their improvement. The interactive whiteboards, SIG training and data analysis were identified as powerful levers for change. However, a number of issues remain unresolved.

The first is one of sustainability as the resources, training, support and financial incentives are removed. Research findings have clearly shown the vulnerability of resource hungry initiatives in the long term (Datnow *et al* 2002) and have pointed to the issue of sustaining activities once the external support and impetus is removed. The second related issue is that of staff turnover, which is already high in these schools but is proving to be particularly the case for those teachers involved in the OCTET project. One of the unintended consequences of equipping teachers with high-level instructional strategies is that they become a very attractive proposition to other schools. The third issue is that of scaling up. The current obsession with scaling up in school reform is based on relatively few examples of success. It is questionable whether scaling up the OCTET process is possible, realistic or even desirable. The intensive way of working with schools is both costly and relatively slow but there are elements of the programme like instructional and emotional training materials that could be distributed to other schools. However, without the associated resource, training and support it is unlikely that these materials will have a significant impact on schools that chose to use them.

Finally, there is the residing powerful issue of external factors that continue to impact negatively upon the school irrespective of its efforts to improve and sustain improvement. Critics of the school effectiveness and school improvement movement have consistently argued that unless the wider social and economic inequities are addressed, schools in challenging circumstances are unlikely to improve (Thrupp 1999; Whitty 2002).

---

4 Whitefield 40%   Channel 12%
   Campion 34%   Phoenix 60%
   The Ridings 20%   Havelock 33%
   Pennywell 32%

They argue that those in the school improvement field are misguided and rather naive if they think their efforts can make any difference against the socio-economic weight of disadvantage that grips schools and their wider communities. They are, of course, right – but only up to a point, as this project has demonstrated. The OCTET project was quite simply an attempt to work collaboratively with teachers, in schools facing considerable and in some cases insurmountable difficulties, to develop new approaches to the teaching and learning. The evaluation evidence and changes in external performance at all of the schools would indicate that the OCTET project was able to mobilize change and to encourage improvements in teaching and learning. How this was achieved however remains a 'school by school' story as each responded in very different ways.

Within the school improvement literature, accounts of programmes, interventions and projects are rarely told by those on the receiving end of them. The literature is replete with neat, rational accounts of school improvement in action and the voices of those involved in the messy implementation process are seldom heard. In contrast, this book offers first-hand accounts of the project in action. These 'tales from the frontline' are intended to offer personal, unique and insightful reflections upon the OCTET project. The heads of the eight schools tell it like it is and remind us what it feels like to be caught up in an external project with its various pressures and demands. Their accounts are therefore particularly valuable for the authentic commentary they offer on the process of improving schools in exceptionally challenging circumstances. The next part of the book provides an account of the OCTET project from the perspective of each of the heads in the project.

References

Datnow, A., Hubbard, L. and Mehan, H. (2002) Extending Educational Reform from One School to Many. London: Falmer Press.

Fullan, M. (1991) *The New Meaning of Educational Change*. London: Cassell.

Fullan, M. (2001) *Leading in a Culture of Change*. San Francisco: Jossey Bass.

Hopkins, D. (2001) *School Improvement for Real*. London: Routledge.

Hopkins, D. and Reynolds, D. (2001) 'The past, present and future of school improvement: towards the Third Age.' *British Educational Research Journal*, Vo. 27, No. 4, 459–75.

Lupton, R. (2004) *Schools in disadvantaged areas: Recognising context and raising performance*. CASE paper 76, London: Centre for Analysis of Social Exclusion, London School of Economics and Political Science.

Reynolds, D. (1998) 'The study and remediation of ineffective schools: some further reflections', in Stolls, L.. and Myers, K. (eds) *No Quick Fixes: Perspectives on Schools in Difficulties*. London: Falmer Press.

Reynolds, D., Clarke, P. and Harris, A. (2004) 'Improving Schools in Exceptionally Challenging Circumstances.' *American Education Research Association Conference*, 11–16 April, San Diego.

Slavin, R. (1996) *Education for All*. Lisse, the Netherlands: Swets & Zeitlinger.

Whitty, G. (2002) *Making Sense of Education Policy*. London: Paul Chapman.

Part 2
The Heads' Tales

3   Campion Catholic High School

Context and background

Campion School serves the three poorest wards in North Liverpool; Everton, Granby and Toxteth. The school was originally formed out of the merger of two Catholic secondary moderns and a Bilateral school. The school is a boys' school with around 550 pupils. Performance in terms of GCSE has been slow but there has been a steady increase, starting from 3%, in 1998, to 5%, 8%, 11%, 15%, 25% and, in 2005, to 34%. The school has a significant number of pupils who come from single-parent families and it draws upon a catchment of high deprivation. The school does not get the full range of ability of pupils as the Head notes: 'There are still a large number of families who will choose to send their pupils to other schools if they can get them in, so we get a very skewed intake in terms of ability.' The school became 11–16 about five years ago and since then rolls have fallen slightly. The school has moved from 660 to the mid-500s.

Unemployment in the area is almost twice the national average at 6.0 per cent; a quarter of this number have never had a job and almost half are long-term unemployed. In terms of all adults, 14.9 per cent are permanently sick or disabled. Altogether, only 30.5 per cent of adults are in work, almost exactly half the national average. Most families (61.3 per cent) live in rented social housing while 13 per cent, more than one in eight, are single parent households with dependent children. The student body is predominantly white mono-ethnic with only 5 per cent of the students from any ethnic minority. More than 60 per cent of pupils are eligible for free school meals and more than 51.5 per cent of the students are officially registered as having special education needs. The school draws its population from its nearest primary school.

Campion is the only secondary school in Liverpool operating within a Parent–School Partnership and to have a dedicated Parents' Centre. This Centre is staffed by a qualified teacher, and functions to support family literacy and family numeracy though the provision, for an audience of parents, of courses and qualifications (for example, the computer 'driving licence') and hopefully to induct parents into the idea of 'lifelong learning' while simultaneously seeking to build parent–school relationships to the benefit of boys' learning. There is also Campion City Learning Centre based just outside the school gates. This was opened in 2001 as part of Liverpool's Education for All initiative and houses nearly 100 computers in several different zones for ICT-based learning, and includes interactive whiteboards and small seminar rooms.

The current head of the school is Tony Phillips who joined the school in 2003. Campion School is staffed by 37 full-time and two part-time teachers who are supported by five teaching and learning assistants. In its Ofsted report (2001) the school was praised for its good teaching, very good leadership and management, and for creating a climate where effective learning and good behaviour was achieved. Despite a history of low attainment in examinations, Campion has never been placed in 'special measures' and similarly it has only officially excluded one student in the last two years.

Ofsted reports have emphasized attainment and attendance as a problem but the school has always been praised for its ethos and its caring community and for the leadership and management within the school. The Head comments:

> in the Ofsted inspection of 1997 all of our feeder schools failed so we can never be complacent here. The school is currently doing a number of things to address those challenges and raise aspirations. Within the school there is a poverty of aspiration – pupils don't value and see the important ladder that education can provide. Because they see second and third-generation unemployment they are less persuaded by the value of qualifications. We've got some pupils at this school – and every school in the country will say the same – who've done massively well with no traditional qualifications. A large number of pupils simply don't buy it and therefore school tries to raise their aspirations.

A recent Ofsted report described the school as being 'an oasis in an area of great deprivation'. The emphasis is upon the successes of pupils who leave and the message to the community is one of raising expectations. Pupils feel that that they're in a safe and stable environment. The Head notes that: 'Challenging schools such as Campion are often expected to take pupils which other schools will not.' In a position of falling roll the pressure to take 'as many kids that we can get' is high. As a result the school often gets persistent non-attendees, pupils who have been removed from other schools and this adds to the problems they face on a daily basis. The Head feels that the staff–pupil ratio is important in challenging schools because of the difficulties associated with dealing with a large number of pupils who are in transition or are simply disaffected with the school.

Campion School has been through a re-structuring of senior management which is now fully in place. The school continues to face the issue of staff recruitment because of its league table position. As the Head notes:

> I've got a fantastic staff here, some young staff, late twenties who've already spent four or five years here and are very keen and willing to stay which I think is brilliant and the staff morale is very high. They're a good working bunch of staff. But when we put adverts in at whatever level, we get very, very few applications, very few because the perception outside schools such as ours – and I'm not speaking specifically of our school now, but the perception is rough school, tough inner-city school.

One of the school's major and persistent challenges is low attainment. Consequently, the reasons for joining the OCTET project were initially to address this issue. In addition there were financial reasons and it was seen as 'a chance for really good in-service for teachers, for really good quality training'. The Head said to staff 'there's seven schools around the country that they've compared – well let's see what their problems are and let's see if we can work together'. It was seen as a chance to collaborate and for professional discussion about school improvement to take place around the country. It was also seen as a chance for people to take advantage of first-class training. The Head notes that the 'SIG training has been excellent. It's made all of the people who've taken part in the project which in our school is everybody actually, feel quite important as well; it's given them a boost of morale as well.'

Initial phase

The expectations of the OCTET project were centrally about raising attainment and securing higher performance.

> I think the staff now have become far more aware of what's out there and what initiatives there are and the importance of data and the analysis of data and learning techniques and teaching styles and things, so in terms of staff development ... and also what's been a boost is that they've also

realized – a number of our staff – that they're ahead of the game in some respects.

The Head's expectation of the project was one of wanting to raise performance: 'It was always at the root of everything and therefore teaching is at the root of everything, so all I've done is continue to emphasize those since I've taken over really.'

The school had a voluntary SIG. There was one member of the senior management in the group but the combination of people was not deliberately engineered.

> We actually have three or four prime movers there and the SIG group came up with ideas, particularly to do with the actual lessons themselves, the style of the lessons, the use of ICT, a lot of these things mesh in together – which have been adopted across the school after full consultation and I think ... I've been very impressed with our SIG group and I intend to keep that group together as a body after the end of the project ... I won't be able to fund exactly everything that we've had in the past, but if I can fund some quality training each year, and give them some time off timetable to develop things for the school I think I'd like to try that. They are empowered, and if they're convinced by something and they can convince me in turn, then we'll do it. I have no problems with supporting them at all.

In addition, there have been significant ICT developments at the school that have been fundamental to the improvement of lessons. ICT is used increasingly across the curriculum and 'these developments were certainly aided by being in the OCTET project along with the extra money and the resources that went into IT training'. HMI reports on the school mention a number of subjects that use technology well within their lessons:

> I've got a Head of Science who presented to the school in January on the use of whiteboards and it was fantastic to see what she can do. The staff went out amazingly enthused. She's got clip art there, she's got web links there and everything showing ... so very impressed with the calibre of some of the work that they're doing.

The OCTET work on data has also benefited the school. There has been a whole-school session on CAT quadrants, including the various learning styles. Heads of department within their planning are asked to refer to where learning styles are actually being used.

The SIG proposed that we should perhaps set a Year 7 group according to the CAT data and then have one sort of almost like study group, control group if you like, of people who have basically the same preferred learning style in a group. That's still under discussion really. I'm neither for or against that at the moment but it needs thinking about.

The initial work undertaken by the SIG looking at learning styles and CAT scores 'was a great catalyst for change'. It was the starting point for reviewing teaching and learning practices in the school. This development has generated self confidence within the SIG group to work with, and to change the practice of, other teachers. This initial work combined with additional resources for ICT meant that the school began to mobilize change around teaching and learning and to look quite critically at classroom practice.

Impact

The Head feels that teachers have seen great benefits from being in the OCTET project. The school has improved greatly and has changed positively.

Staff feel that they are doing well, that they've changed their teaching techniques and they can see the benefits. The most important change for this school I would say is teaching and learning. What I like is the solidity of our staff ... we've now got two or three generations of staff here driving things on so that's encouraging.

HMI reported a high proportion of good lessons, better than satisfactory lessons and a very, very small proportion of unsatisfactory during the developmental phase of the OCTET project. This would suggest that pupils are getting a better range of teaching approaches in the classroom. However, it is clear that while pupils have recognized a change, they would not associate the changes with the project. 'If I were to mention "OCTET" to 100 pupils they wouldn't have a clue what you're talking about.' The Head notes that 'The power of the project lies in its various elements that include more interactive whiteboards and concentrated staff development that has focused on teaching and learning.'

The Head feels that OCTET has had a significant impact on pupils' attainment and performance.

Absolutely! Oh absolutely! In every subject I would say it has changed its delivery for the pupils and I think lots of lessons are ... I mean I'm humbled by seeing – I'm very impressed with young teachers, the styles of teaching they use – it makes me feel even older than I am, so I'm very impressed with them so I think there's been an impact for the students and the staff.

The Head's role throughout the project has been one of working with teachers but particularly to work with the SIG and to sit down with them 'once a term, and ask them for an update on developments or their latest training and ask them for recommendations about how to disseminate new work within the school'.

The SIG have been instrumental in training events within the school. The group ran regular INSET sessions for staff and ran a market place where every department was given three tables and every department had to bring up an example of a piece of work that they've introduced as a direct result of OCTET, a direct result of SIG.

It could be a whole lesson plan, it could be a section of a lesson – the plenary or the starter activity whatever it was, or a card game, things that they may be using or whatever, it didn't matter what it was. But they then had to put on display for all the teachers to then go around and see what all the other departments are doing. One of our cynical old teachers, and there are only a few, said to me on the next day he said, 'You know that INSET we had yesterday, that was the best we've had for years, you shouldn't bother getting people in, we should use our own staff.'

There was an expectation very early on in the project that the SIG would contribute to whole-school development. Given that the SIG went away for six days a year meeting people from other schools there was an expectation that when they returned they would work with staff to share their learning. The impact of having seven teachers out of a school with only 39 staff in total inevitably placed a strain upon the school, hence it was expected that the SIG would deliver high-quality feedback.

I'm fully supportive of continuing professional development, we all should be, but I think if they're out of school for a couple of days, the school should have something back. Whether it's a presentation by them for an hour or so in next INSET or whatever I don't mind but somehow this has got to cascade back into the institution.

The Head feels that the combination of pressure from HMI and support from the OCTET project allowed the school to move forward in a productive way but that there were inevitable tensions along the way. Where OCTET helped was by providing a network of people that could offer support, advice and practical help to relieve the tension. As a result of OCTET the Head feels the school is more accountable for what it does: 'I think schools generally feel accountable, but I think the schools in the OCTET project have felt especially accountable.'

However, this pressure at times has proved too great:

> The HMI visits we've had every year were very draining on staff, very. What I'd say to the DfES is that the school has never been in special measures, never been in serious weaknesses, yet the staff were made to feel like they were. Even though the reports were very positive the process placed an enormous cost and strain on the staff.

Overall, the Head feels that teachers have seen great benefits from being in the OCTET project. The school has improved greatly and has changed positively. 'Staff feel that they are doing well, that they've changed their teaching techniques and they can see the benefits. Most important change for this school I would say is teaching and learning.'

Reflections

There are strategies from the project that the Head feels can work to improve other schools in challenging circumstances. The first is a concentration on learning styles. The OCTET focus on CAT scores and associated learning styles was considered to be a success by the school and allowed teachers to focus directly on teaching and learning styles. The second strategy is quality training provision, as the training provided by the OCTET project was considered particularly effective. The third strategy is effective management and leadership in schools, particularly at the middle leader level. The fourth strategy is building community in its widest sense by ensuring teachers work with teachers and the school works with parents. As the Head notes:

> Schools in better circumstances sometimes don't have a collaborative approach but a collegiate staff is essential to school improvement. Because our staff work together tremendously well and they've been a great support to me over the last couple of years as well. But there are some schools in

Liverpool that I know of where staff morale is not as high perhaps, because they don't work together.

The school's current priorities are attendance and behaviour management. The priorities for the future will remain those of continuing to raise attainment and sustaining improvement. A key priority for the school is to consider vocational alternatives and the Head feels that there are changes at Key Stage 4 that the school can and should make. The school has introduced more ICT for the pupils and is introducing media studies. There are students on college placements, the school offers nautical studies for 16-year-olds and there are a range of charitable institutions involved with the school. The aspiration of the school is to redress the 'tail of disaffection' and to 'engage more pupils'. The Head notes:

> I wouldn't like to put a percentage on our disaffection, but disaffection is there to be seen. It shows itself in poor attendance: in some cases we have 10% missing and we have a large number of pupils who other schools will not take and some of those are pupils who didn't go to junior school. For example we've got 14 pupils who don't do any exams, yet our league table is based on the 120, not the 106 who come in.

As a consequence the Head would like to see the school coping with the disaffection better than it does at the moment, but inevitably this implies greater resource.

Reflecting on the OCTET project, the Head feels that working with a group of schools with a broadly similar attainment level 'was a very liberating experience'.

> The recent policy agenda from the DFES about collaboration is one which I have total support for. The experience of OCTET is one which has shown that managers at all levels whether head of department, whether it's senior managers, whether it's headteachers can learn from working with colleagues facing the same challenges. As a small school the OCTET project was embraced by everybody and everybody was on board. This was very positive plus the fact that the SIG were teachers who were well respected in the staff room and that joining the group was voluntary. I do think the make up of the SIG is crucial – that the people who are involved in improvement need time, resources, good training, they need to be released from school perhaps four or five times a year as group – perhaps a small

group of four or five – some schools can't manage eight or nine – with the expectation that we get something back from it, that they should feel empowered and they should have the support of management. If they haven't got the confidence of management there's no point in having them. So that's what makes the composition and make-up of it critical.

It is clear from the OCTET experience that every single change in the school cannot be driven by the Head alone; it requires broad partici-pation in the school improvement process. The OCTET project brought change to 35 classrooms and therefore had to be owned by the staff group and not senior management.

If it is owned and driven by the staff they'll take it on board and my job in that sense has been to facilitate that really, no more than that, and sit back and slightly marvel at the fact that they do it a lot better than I could. What's impressed my staff I think is that the SIG members a) have had an enjoyable time because they've networked with people from other schools, but b) they've worked hard and have shown other staff what they've done and therefore the staff I think appreciate that and think 'They're not telling me to do more work than they're doing themselves' so they're leading by example really.

As the school's results have gone up, staff have been able to see progress from their involvement with OCTET but they do not underestimate the difficulties that remain.

What you've got to realize is that our school is challenged from above and below. We are in the middle of a challenge vice with expectations from above, to perform and from below because of the context in which we work.

However, the Head feels that the OCTET project has contributed to rising standards of attainment at GCSE and

better teaching, better classroom, better lessons, better examples of teaching and learning across the school. Success breeds success really and I think some of our teachers now have begun to see success. Their efforts have been noted, inspected, evaluated and they've seen some results in their exam performance as well.

In the longer term, the Head hopes that the school can begin to redress some of the inbalance in intake and that gradually parents will realize that this school has got as much, if not more, to offer than others. Long term it is hoped that teachers themselves realize what they can do in the classroom to improve a) their delivery and b) the experience for the pupils. In short, the aim is to sustain improvement and to continue to work in ways that build the internal capacity for productive change and development.

4 Channel School

Context and background

The Channel School is situated on the outskirts of Folkestone, Kent, on the south coast. It is a mixed 11–16 high school with 790 students on roll in the summer of 2003. Its roll has shown a steady increase since at least 1997. The 1999 Ofsted report noted that 96 per cent of the students at The Channel School are white and only 11 pupils were from homes where English is not the first language. In March 2002, HMI found that there were 21 pupils from the families of asylum seekers. In addition, the school has accepted children who have had to leave other schools in the region and in March 2002, the total number of children admitted after the start of term was 59. In March 2002, the school's HMI reported that 'of the 827 pupils on roll, 67 per cent are on the register of special educational needs'. HMI noted in March 2002 that about one third of pupils were entitled to free school meals, which is approximately twice the national average.

The Channel School is one of six secondary schools in the area. There are two grammar schools, three foundation schools and the Channel School. The others are foundation schools that opted to be grant maintained. These schools have entrance examinations which has gradually shifted the balance of the intake so that almost 60 per cent of the intake at Channel is on the Special Needs register. A vast proportion of these children have behavioural and emotional problems and the school is located in the most challenging area of Folkestone. Also the Head notes the school suffers from the fact that 'children themselves feel almost from day one that they are failures. The comment I heard most when I first came to this school last year was "Why have you bothered coming here? This is a rubbish school and we're thick!"'

The school serves a very large, predominantly white, estate with a high percentage of single parent families. Very few parents have professional or semi-professional qualifications, or had any experience of further or higher education. In the last couple of years external factors have worked against Folkestone, such as the building of the Channel Tunnel which meant the loss of the ferry service. In addition, the M20 motorway means that Folkestone is now by-passed, plus there are no large-scale employers apart from SAGA in the area. Understandably the school serves a community with very low aspirations.

On all of the external performance criteria, the school under-performs although the latest PANDA data shows that the school provides considerable added value from Key Stages 2 to 3; however, until this year, this has not been sustained from Key Stages 3 to 4. Literacy is a major problem: over 70 per cent of the pupils entering the school are operating with literacy and numeracy levels below their chronological age and the school is looking very hard at ways in which it can improve pupil literacy levels. In addition, many of the staff have been teaching in this school or similar schools for a long time which can affect their expectations of pupils: 'I think that some staff had quite low expectations of the pupils', says the headteacher. In October 2002 the school was placed in special measures. The Head notes: 'I don't think that until you're in the situation of being in special measures you can ever fully comprehend what that pressure is like and how much tunnel vision it creates.' The school, however, came out of special measures in June 2004 and achieved the best examination results, 21% A*–C grades in the same year. In 2005 its GCSE results increased to 22%.

Initial phase

At the start of the project in September 2001, the school was led by the team which included Bob Fox as Head and Martin Locke as his Deputy. They had been appointed in 1994 at a time when the school was at a very low ebb. In 1996 the school came out of its first episode of 'special measures' and in the following two years there were signs that the turbulence of the early 1990s had been overcome. In 2003 Colette Singleton was appointed as Head.

The school was included in the OCTET project because it was in extremely challenging circumstances and thought to be a school that was well led and well managed. However, when the new Head arrived there was a great deal of resentment about the OCTET project from staff because they believed that it was the cause of them being placed in special measures. The Head notes that while OCTET was, in principle, something that was 'really good', the foundations simply were not there to support the project or the development work that it required. So the Head feels that in some respect OCTET was a 'lost opportunity because', as she says, 'I don't think the way in which the money was spent, the way in which support was targeted in actual fact supported the school. I think it was used in ways that almost undermined the school.'

The Head strongly subscribes to one of the main principles reflected in the OCTET project, which is improving the quality of teaching and learning.

> I know there were people here initially who thought that if I, 'she', would just sort out the behaviour of the children everything would be wonderful and I keep hammering home the fact that many of the problems that we have with behaviour are to do with the quality of the teaching and learning.

Consequently, the school has had a major focus on teaching and learning. One of the things the Head did immediately was to make the SIG a lot smaller and bring some new people into the group to reflect a better gender balance and representation across subjects. Since this change the SIG has begun to impact positively upon teaching and learning within the school. The SIG has been used to deliver training and the emphasis has been on modelling the sorts of lessons that are most effective. 'We've done lots of "back to basics": the three-part lesson, learning objectives, the use of starters, plenaries, inter-active activities, group work, that sort of thing.' This approach is obviously working as the data from the HMI visits is demonstrating that the percentage of satisfactory and especially good and very good lessons is growing all the time. However, the Head adds: 'We've got a number of people who are still teaching for control, because of the behaviour of the youngsters.' In the last inspection visit over half the lessons inspected were considered good or very good.

There has also been an emphasis on developing middle management as this is considered to be a weak area in the school.

> We've got a number of very young or relatively inexperienced middle managers. Unfortunately, for various reasons, the middle management training delivered through the OCTET project actually worked against the school because, of the three people who went, two of them resigned because they said they weren't prepared to do those things and they left the school.

The school has now developed its own home-grown middle management training which takes place every other week and is hosted each time by a different department. Every meeting has three clear parts: the first provides an opportunity for the host department to showcase something that they do well in order to share good practice; second, there is a maintenance /information section; and third there is a developmental section. For example, every department by the end of this year will have a handbook that will have been worked through, section by section, around an agreed format with everybody supporting each other. The Head notes that the work with middle managers would have taken place irrespective of the project, 'but this work has certainly developed the capacity of our middle managers by enabling them to understand what their role actually is and giving them the skills to carry it out more effectively'.

While the school has achieved a lot through its middle management training, the impact of ICT developments have proved to be much slower. The video conferencing equipment, due to technical reasons, has had no impact whereas the move to purchase interactive whiteboards has been far more successful. At the moment the school has 30 whiteboards which means almost all classrooms have this facility. In addition, most teachers now have laptops, which are a further part of the strategy to use ICT in teaching and learning in a much more strategic and integral way.

The OCTET project also introduced a new way of working with data. Initially two factors worked against this initiative – the data proved difficult to use for technical reasons and the data manager didn't fully understand how to use it. The appointment of a new data manager, the resolution of some of the glitches and support from the LEA now means that staff are beginning to develop a greater expertise and confidence in the use of data. Teachers are becoming more used to CAT data and the mapping of quadrant data to learning styles is having a beneficial effect on learning.

> It's helping us with grouping of children and looking at strategies that we use to actually teach them which raised awareness of some of the challenges. Now people have got very simple data packs which are useable and HMI have commented very favourably on the way staff are using the quadrant data to meet the learning needs of the pupils.

Literacy levels, as already highlighted, are an issue at the school. Unfortunately the project's literacy initiative, the RML programme, was met with some resistance, particularly from the then Head of the Pupil Support Unit. The Head notes:

I was informed, in no uncertain terms, by the Head of Pupil Support that neither she nor any of her LSAs were going to be involved in this training and that she'd already told people that this was the case. Unfortunately that soured the whole thing, which was a shame as we did have one member of the English department who actually worked on it and quite liked it as a programme. But because it was very much located just in one department, and there was no real understanding across the school about what the approach was trying to do, or any real attempt to bring it through into other areas, I think it just withered on the vine.

When the current Head first came to the school she saw the OCTET project as

another way in which we could move the school forward. I don't think I fully understood until I came here just what the issues were. This was not a school where nothing had been tried; there was evidence that there had been some attempts at looking at teaching and learning and there had certainly been a lot of strategies as far as managing the behaviour of the youngsters were concerned, but none of them seemed to have had any lasting impact.

The Head felt that there was every danger that the OCTET project could go the same way.

The Head's main expectations of the project were to provide external support and new ideas, but she found coming into the project late inevitably placed her at a disadvantage.

I came too late into the project to develop the sorts of relationships that I think you need with your fellow heads. It's not that they weren't welcoming, they were, they were very supportive, but I wasn't able to leave the school to develop those relationships and access that support. You can't be a caretaker head in a school like this, you've got to be here every single day. I've missed that; I've missed the freedom to go out and to meet other people, to talk to other people and to share ideas.

The financial contribution of the project proved to be helpful because it enabled the school to try new things and develop new materials. Initially, part of the problem the Head faced was that a great deal of the money was tied into staff salaries and while the adult–pupil ratio was quite low the net gains were not reflected in teaching and learning. 'Around the school there were lots of support staff but it didn't seem to be making any difference, it wasn't improving the quality of what was going on in the classrooms, it wasn't raising standards.' Consequently, a restructuring of staffing to release some of the funding was undertaken, and has been shown to be successful.

Impact

In considering the impact of the project the Head feels that one of the most beneficial aspects of it was the SIG training: 'I think that was good for them. It was good for them to go out and meet teachers from other schools, it was good for them to hear and to share new ideas.' The SIG training gave members an opportunity to talk to other teachers with different perceptions of the project and allowed them to get a better sense of its purposes and aims. The Head is in no doubt that the SIG has played 'a significant role in the drive to improve teaching and learning'. One major frustration, also shared by other schools, was the fact that the video conferencing did not work and the opportunities to link with schools outside the SIG training did not materialize.

Early in the project the Head created a new leadership team and decided to go for a slightly flatter structure. Five assistant heads were appointed, some in subjects where additional support was needed and all were people who were good role models 'as far as teaching and learning was concerned'. Some of the assistant heads and the Head have had quite a heavy involvement with the SIG.

> Initially I tended to be very involved with the group, simply because I'm passionate as I said about teaching and learning. More recently I've handed that role over more to the two assistant heads with responsibility for teaching and learning, and I think I'm going to have to do a bit of careful bridge-building there because I don't think it's been quite as successful as it might have been. I think it's just people – new people, new approaches maybe with not quite the understanding of the journey that other people have taken so far. So there's a need to revisit that area.

However, as a school that was in special measures at that time, there were extra demands on staff and constraints which other schools did not experience.

> One of the interesting things about being in a school like this in the current situation, is you have absolutely no delusions about what has to be done – it's in your face the whole time. HMI are in regularly. They pull no

punches and they tell you exactly what's wrong with the school – and, virtually every 11 weeks, they're back again wanting to see progress and tangible results from their last visit.

In gauging the impact of the project the Head points towards the school's successful exit from special measures which was achieved in less than 18 months. In addition, the school culture has shifted along with children's expectations of themselves, the community's expectation of them and teachers' expectations. For many years the tacit understanding between staff and pupils was 'you don't bother me and I don't bother you' and now this has radically changed. In 2006 the school will become an academy and it is hoped that these positive cultural changes will remain.

> Lots of people comment on the fact that when they walk round the school that now it's much calmer and the youngsters, on the whole, are in lessons. Obviously you get a few hot spots at times, but there's a much more positive feel about the school. I've worked hard to improve the quality of the environment, which with the poor quality of the buildings has not been very easy, but we've put a lot of money into developing a new dining room, a maths suite, a new business room etc., installing interactive whiteboards and improving the numbers of computers in all the computer rooms so that every child can now sit and work at a computer and they don't have to share.

Reflections

Looking back on the OCTET project and its influence upon the school, the current Head feels that the pace of change has often proved to be too slow. While the project has undoubtedly contributed to improvements in the school a big frustration for the Head is that the project started at a point where the school was so much further back than it is today. The Head has actively tried to move the school forward by creating teams and relying on others to work together.

> I try in every way that I can, in little ways and big ways to give people practical support, the input that they need to try and improve the situation. What I cannot do – and I keep saying this to them – is I cannot change the profile of the children in this school. This is The Channel School and the bottom line is, you either choose to work here or you don't. I can't do it on my own, we can only achieve things by working as a team.

Recruitment is becoming more and more of an issue at the school and as the Head notes:

> Schools like this need the availability of really good staff willing to work in challenging schools like this. And when they are, they're brilliant, they're fantastic I cannot fault them, but certainly in some subject areas even the grammar schools are having difficulty getting staff. Obviously in schools like ours it is even more challenging. At a time when we've got staffing shortages across the country people have said to me, 'Why on earth should I want to work in a school like this?'

Parents also have commented positively on the development and improvement of the school. The school has done quite a lot of work on gifted and talented children, particularly involving parents of the children in Key Stage 3.

> We've reintroduced parents' evenings because they'd stopped those, we've had Raising Achievement Evenings for the Year 11 and the Year 9 students, and people are saying that, yes, they are seeing a difference, but it's slow.

The school sends out a newsletter three or four times a term to keep people informed and on Thursdays the Head runs a surgery where parents can just phone in and arrange a meeting. This has proved to be successful and has improved communication with parents.

> I think community perception is very difficult to change and again it's something we will be focusing on much, much more in the future when we've got a bit more space. It's something we're working on at the moment, but we need to put much more effort into that I think.

The OCTET project's relentless emphasis on high-quality teaching and learning has contributed to a more positive learning culture at the school. In addition, the Head has reinforced that everyone is a leader whether it's within their classrooms, within their departments or within their sphere pastorally or academically. The school now pays more attention to the power of the student voice. A student council has been introduced with very clear structures to operate in: 'They have a budget, they're responsible for being part of the process of selecting staff, they do a presentation each term to the governing body. I think involving pupils is imperative to bringing about improvement. Pupils need to feel valued and that their voice is heard.'

In 2006 when the school will become an academy, a new principal will be appointed to lead the new school. The current Head therefore has been working on areas which the new academy will encompass and has been anticipating new developments such as ICT.

> A major focus naturally in those fantastic new buildings will be on ICT as a platform for learning within the academy, so that's why we've moved towards the interactive whiteboards. Obviously, apart from the fact that it's the way to go, I want the staff here who want to move into the academy to be as ICT literate as they possibly can be. To demonstrate that they're using ICT effectively and the youngsters are used to it. I want to introduce notebooks around the school, suites of laptops in cabinets so that staff can use them in lessons as a natural part of what they do and as a new approach to teaching and learning.

Looking back on the experience, the advice the Head would want to give to other headteachers in challenging circumstances would be first, to develop a good team to take developmental work forward, and second, to have the courage to know that maybe the Head is not always the best person to lead an initiative.

> You appoint people or create a team where in a sense you are an entity and entirety as a team because you all have skills and strengths and as a head you have to play to those. At the same time you have to know when there are people on the team that can do things better that you. But you also know that there are times when you have to step back, even when you know you would do it differently, and let them do it the way that they want to do it. It's about having courage and humility. I also think you have to have a sense of humour, especially when things go wrong!

Third, there needs to be the right blend of the practical and the theoretical.

> It's not enough just to be practical; you also have to have a theoretical understanding that underpins so much of the decision-making, so you've got to be … you've got to read and be alive the whole time; you've got to change yourself I suppose, you've got to be willing yourself to acknowledge new ideas and be aware of what's happening. And that's quite difficult actually because there is so much change going on, to be abreast of everything, isn't always easy. But you've got to create that enquiring spirit within your team, within your staff, within your students. After all if schools are institutions of learning we should all be learners.

Finally, you've got to believe in the worth and the value of what you've doing, even on the darkest days. I don't know what motivates other people, I suppose it's different things that motivate everybody, but I personally don't think I could do a job like this just for financial reward, or status – and I'm not suggesting for one moment that other people do it for those reasons. But I think if those were the only motivational factors, I think it would be very difficult to continue to do a job like this.

5 Havelock School

Context and background

Havelock School is a mixed comprehensive 11–16 school on the outskirts of Grimsby. Havelock is in the unitary authority of NE Lincolnshire which is a very small LEA, and consequently adviser support is limited. The traditional catchment area for the school is the north east ward, which is the old fishing community of Grimsby. The ward is one of the most deprived in the country. Unemployment at 6.8 per cent is twice the national average and more than 10 per cent of all households in Heneage are single parent households with dependent children. The geographical position of Havelock School (on the edge of its catchment area) presents problems with its relationship with the community, since the pupils tend to live some way away from the school. In 1997, 43 per cent of the pupils were entitled to free school meals. In 2003, the number had dropped to 36 per cent and 25 per cent of students were reported as having special educational needs. Concerns have been raised in successive Ofsted reports about the low attainment levels on entry, and low performance in national tests.

At the beginning of the 1980s, two schools in the ward were closed, and pupils transferred to Havelock School; at this time there were over 1,200 students at the school, including a thriving sixth form. However, in 1990 there was a school reorganization and, like other Grimsby schools, Havelock lost their sixth form. The consequence of this for Havelock School was a falling roll which reduced to its lowest level of 500 pupils. These circumstances placed the school in a position of serious disadvantage because of strong competition from the neighbouring schools. In the view of the current headteacher, Jane Dyer, 'the school was languishing'. The resulting academic performance was 'catastrophically bad' and there were very few pockets of good practice in teaching and learning. The school suffered a very high turnover of staff, a high turnover of pupils and their performance historically hovered around 8% gaining five A*–C GCSE grades. Consequently, the school became unpopular, and parents sent their pupils elsewhere. Havelock was achieving only 6% A*–Cs in the late 1990s. The previous headteacher had been in post for 14 years, and improvement had already begun when Jane Dyer, previously the Deputy Head and then Acting Head, became the Head in April 2000.

Staffing issues have been, and remain, a major concern at Havelock School. Grimsby's geographical position exacerbates the difficulties in recruiting teachers. A shortage of applicants can lead either to appointments which are not of the highest quality, or to having to leave the post unfilled. An example of the seriousness of staff shortages on key departments is shown in the fact that three science teachers left in July 2002. Eleven staff left during the school year 2003–04. Staff recruitment costs are high, and are a significant drain on the budget. Part of the school's difficulties were caused by acute financial difficulties when Jane Dyer took over and the school was in great need of serious refurbishment. She notes: 'There is a traditional attachment to the school, with parents saying "We went there and our children will go there".' However, despite this attachment there remains a relative disinterest from parents in the school and in academic achievement. In addition, the school had attracted a disproportionate number of pupils with special educational needs and students excluded from other schools, since the school has a good reputation for supporting difficult young people. These situations have skewed Havelock's overall pupil profile, and have had a negative impact on the school's performance and position in the league tables.

When Jane Dyer joined the school, it was approaching the first of the two Ofsted inspections and her remit as a deputy was to improve Key Stage 3 performance and to increase pupil numbers. Following a good Ofsted inspection the positive advances made at the school were quickly reversed because of significant demographic changes and a deteriorating employment profile in Grimsby. The declining fishing industry led to a changing demographic profile and the rise of unemployment in the area. Gradually, this changing profile altered the social mix of the pupil intake and in addition the possibilities of parents choosing the school were limited and remain so by local boundaries. As the Head outlines: 'The school boundaries have been demarked in such a way that does not help the school. One of the good and rising primaries is actually on our playing field yet they are not designated to come to us!'

In summary, prior to joining the OCTET project Havelock School faced a wide range of external and internal related issues that made improving performance particularly difficult. The attitudes of both staff and pupils were less than optimum and expectations of achievement were poor. In the build-up to joining the OCTET project, there was a general prevailing culture of low expectations. However, in the view of the Head, 'These low expectations were not the fault of staff or the pupils – the local area holds a poor view of education.' It was evident that improving standards at the school was directly linked to improving community perceptions of the school and the Head acknowledged that she had 'a key role to play in this endeavour'.

As noted earlier, the school is in receipt of a significant number of pupils who are socially deprived and under supported. In 2004, for example, of 160 pupils in the current Year 11, only 38 were estimated to be in a position of achieving five A*–C GCSE grades. Fifteen pupils in this cohort are no longer living at home. The Head notes:

> There are children sleeping on camp beds in the homes of their near relations who at worst are mingling with disreputable youths who are in unmanaged accommodation. There are multiple marriages and broken relationships. Newly constituted families are pushing children out far too early and huge rows ensue and the children are significantly underprotected, and undernourished.

Initial stages

The school was invited to join the OCTET project along with the seven other schools at an introductory meeting in London. This meeting had a particularly dramatic affect on the school staff as the Head recalls:

> I can remember coming back from London, going into the staff room, explaining that not only had we got the opportunity but we'd got money to support it and that it was a long-term project, and the effect on the staff was just dramatic, it was stunning to behold. They'd been noticed, they'd got help and support and it really was quite a remarkable meeting.

Early on the school publicized their involvement in the OCTET project by putting a whole range of newspaper articles and mail shots together in an attempt to attract parental interest. The school delivered mail shots and prospectuses to individual homes explaining that the school was very different and how being involved in the project meant they were starting afresh. Initially parents were very sceptical but the determination of staff to make a difference under the banner of OCTET meant that the school kept on trying to involve and engage parents. The Head notes: 'Being in the OCTET project has helped us market the school very, very success-fully and we have luxuriated in that.'

The chance to be involved in a first-class national project was considered to be 'a real opportunity' by most staff at the school. Most teachers were immensely positive about the possibilities of the project as the Head describes: 'It gave us the opportunity to really re-write what we wanted to do at the school.' The Head is in no doubt that the OCTET project will continue to bring dividends in results in the next three or four years and that the project represents long-term and sustainable change.

The Head's initial expectations about the project focused on the fact that 'it could be a real lever for change with the staff'. She felt that it provided an important marketing opportunity for change with significant resources attached. It offered the opportunity for teachers to access high-quality training with other teachers from schools in similar circum-stances. The Head's expectations were those 'of raising standards, raising the stakes, increasing the speed of change, attracting a different calibre of staff and attracting a different cohort of pupils'.

Initially the OCTET project focus was very much on developing the eight Heads and working through networks and teams. The Head reflects: 'In its own right, it was a marvellous and extremely useful basis for talking to other very supportive colleagues and I am indebted to them.' But on a broader basis, the networking between schools soon started to pay dividends as ideas flowed between the schools. Training for middle managers and the development of the SIG were initially viewed positively, although it was acknowledged that taking staff out during the working school day was very difficult to manage.

The Head's initial experience of the OCTET project was positive. She enjoyed the interaction and support of headteacher colleagues, colleagues from DfES and LEA personnel. In addition, it was her view that teachers were being given 'first-class training and the opportunity to make a real and immediate difference for children'. The Head ensured that both staff and pupils were informed about the project. There were pupil assem-blies which focused on the changes the school was making. The Head notes that the 'Pupils really enjoyed the fact that visitors from central government were coming to see us and we tried to make it very special for them.'

However, in the initial stages not all aspects of the OCTET project were so positive. There were frustrations with the progress of the assessment work and the pace at which the training sessions for the SIG commenced. Yet, it was evident that once operational, the SIG training was an important component of the project's success. The Head notes:

> The SIG training has been instrumental in moving the school forward. If I was to pick one aspect of the project, that would be it. And again, I know I'm not alone in this. It has given a diverse group of staff the opportunity to work together, it's developed their confidence and their competence, it's enabled them to take a lead in staff development across the school and they've done this with a very sound voice and it's been extremely well received. So I think that's absolutely first class as a development and something that will nourish us in the years to come because it's given us a mechanism to use the very positive aspects of the school to self-evaluate, self-heal and move on.

In terms of ICT, the school was already in a very fortunate position because of the fact that they were in an Educational Action Zone. The Education Action Zone had a particular focus on improving ICT so the school was able, with the help of OCTET, to bring together the two developments. This equipped the school with an interactive whiteboard in every teaching room and provided all staff with their own portable computer to generate high-quality teaching resources. The result of this development was to make teachers 'rethink what they were doing'. In addition, it raised expectations of teaching and learning for pupils. The Head cites the example of pupils in one particular English group who signed a petition for their teacher to have a whiteboard:

> They felt so strongly about this, that in the end I had to give in because they were essentially claiming the right to high-quality teaching and they wouldn't relent! So they had to have one – so thank you OCTET. It is quite incredible the difference that's they have made to teaching and learning and we intend to develop that even further.

The training days run by the SIG team following the SIG training events were considered to be 'absolutely inspirational and a delight to be at'. It was evident that the ideas had been really 'taken on board' because teachers were keen to deliver training to other teachers at their own school.

Impact

The impact of the project can be gauged in a number of ways.
Examination results have improved at the school and in 2005 the school
achieved 20% A*–C GCSE grades. Another indicator of success has been
the re-establishment of the school within the wider community. This has
been evident most recently in the increase in student numbers. As the
Head outlines: 'The school has virtually doubled in size and that is really
quite astounding given the demographic decline in the local area, so that's
a great joy to us.'

Other signals of positive change in the school have included improved
recruitment and retention of teachers and an enhanced staff profile
in terms of teaching capability and expertise. There is a new sense of
'collective morale' at the school that has manifested itself in a changed
view of the school insofar that it is much more positive and forward
looking. As the Head acknowledged:

> Certainly there was a change in perceptions about this school from other
> local schools ... we had training opportunities and our very, very positive
> Ofsted suggested that we were doing exceptionally well in staff devel-
> opment and in our quality of teaching.

The Head advocates that looking at different teaching and learning
styles was a very critical turning point for the school. Primarily, this was
because teachers were put in a position where they were analysing the
quality of their teaching and reflecting upon how to improve this further.
The focus on 'teaching and learning' promoted by the project was an
important lever for change as it allowed teachers to share good practice
and to try new approaches in the classroom.

The Head's role in the project was very much one of setting the vision
and establishing new standards and higher expectations. In her view it
was essential to 'capture the enthusiasm and interest of the staff, enabling
them and empowering them to move things forward'. Throughout the
project the Head was a constant driving force for change and maintained
the pressure for improvement, despite the movement of staff and significant changes in the SIG membership.

The major achievements identified by the school, so far, can be summarized as 're-focusing attention upon an educational agenda and ensuring
that the school is making a difference to the life chances of young people'.

The school is currently working as a team to continue to raise standards. The Head recognizes the contribution made by OCTET both personally and professionally:

> OCTET has given the staff the opportunity to work with a group of professionals who've shown similar enthusiasm about school improvement. Essentially, it's about capturing that enthusiasm and luring people to make that change – sometimes against their will, but usually with their support. So I'm very lucky to be Head here and I'm very lucky with the colleagues I have. The OCTET project and associated funding gave the school prestige which has to be a very good thing.

The impact of OCTET at Havelock School has been fourfold:

- pupil numbers have increased to nearly double in the last three years;
- the public perception of the school appears to be much more positive and there is greater community support;
- the examination results have improved;
- the improvement trajectory for the school is set in an upward trend based on new curriculum development.

Reflections

On reflection the Head believes that teachers in the school have changed and are now 'highly committed to a process of excellent staff development and support'. Pupils also seem to have changed in their attitudes to learning. They are now very acutely aware of different learning styles, and, as the Head notes, 'They're quite self-critical about it as well'. In addition, parents' perceptions of the school have shifted significantly in the last three years, as there are now more pupils entering Years 7 and 8 than in previous years.

In summary, the Head believes that OCTET has been successful at Havelock School because it raised expectations about what was possible. It has achieved this through making staff interested in classroom innovation and improving the quality of teaching and learning. The success of the project, in the view of the Head, has been 'its focus quality on creating high calibre; highly motivated, single-minded teachers who make a tremendous difference'. In the future the school is considering seeking specialist status in the area of technology to further enhance and consolidate improvements in teaching and learning.

> The development of ICT is particularly instrumental in my thinking because it encompasses every aspect of the curriculum, so for us it would be a much better status for us to go for than any others I can think of.

However, the Head's ambition for the school is to achieve a stable level of improvement:

> Ideally I would like to see the school in a position where it is secure. It may plateau with its examination results, but I mean a secure, sound base where the quality of teaching and learning is consistently good.

Overall the Head's ambition for the school 'is to serve the natural catchment area' and to ensure that 'more aspiring families choose Havelock for their children'. There is clearly a marked change in pupil entry at the school, but the Head recognizes that there is more work to be done to consolidate this position. In reflecting on the achievements of the school and the impact of the OCTET project, the Head concludes that:

> All things are possible and we do have to be positive in challenging circumstances. I think that staff training and development is a key tool in both the retention and raising standards agendas. Good quality training has made us able to recruit new teachers as the existing staff have talked positively about their experiences in the project and at the school. They talk to their friends, to other teachers and they talk to the families of these children. This has proved to be a very powerful tool for recruitment and improvement.

In terms of advice to other schools, the Head reflects:

> One has to stay true to one's vision as a Head and the route to school improvement had got to be an attainable goal and sometimes it may be very small steps but you should never lose sight of it. Teachers want to get it right, they want to make a difference, they want children to improve, they care about the individual child and the school and the results and that they are desperately disheartened in challenging schools when they are made to feel that they are not delivering whereas the reality of the situation is the fact that my colleagues are working very hard, and should be praised not criticized.

The Head acknowledges that the route to school improvement in a school in extremely challenging circumstances is far from easy. The strain of reaching over 25% of five A*–C GCSE grades for some schools can be a very daunting target and it is clear that external factors can make that more or less of a real possibility. But from the Head of Havelock School there is some clear advice about reaching that possibility: 'Listen, learn and choose the route to improvement carefully but never forget your vision because that's the essential part of making a difference.'

6   Pennywell School

Context and background

Pennywell School is an 11–16 mixed comprehensive school, located on the Pennywell estate. This estate is a high crime-risk area and there is a permanent police post on the estate. Crindon, the ward in which the school is located, is mono-ethnic: 98.8 per cent of the population is white. There has been a recent influx of asylum seekers which has caused some ethnic tensions. Unemployment is a major concern in the area. Only 6.4 per cent of the 9.548 registered residents of Grindon ward are officially unemployed (and seeking work), and another 12.9 per cent are permanently sick or disabled. The statistics show that 47 per cent of Pennywell adults had been unemployed for over 12 months, and 39 per cent for more than two years. Shipbuilding and mining within the area have been replaced by call centres and car-making as the major source of employment.

Since the late 1990s, there have been increasing problems with the recruitment and retention of staff at the school. Pennywell has had to use supply teachers to fulfil teaching roles though as the present Head, Pat Pattison, says: 'Supply teachers don't work at a school like Pennywell.' Sixteen staff left the school at the end of the 2000–01 school year (and were replaced in part by 14 NQTs in September 2001); another 16 staff left (including a deputy head) at the end of the 2002–03 school year. The emerging profile is one where new teachers come and stay for two years and then move on. Staff tend to move around the local area of the North East so a local reputation is important and beneficial. The fact that teachers have succeeded at Pennywell is a major recommendation for their next post.

The school is a social centre for the community and there are few other such centres in the immediate surrounding area. There is extensive use of Pennywell's facilities by the local population. Pennywell is a designated Community School with an adult education programme which includes vocational training and qualifications such as GNVQ. Less than half the students (45%) have special education needs and 54% are eligible for free school meals. There is a 'curriculum access provision' for 35 statemented pupils taught in the mainstream. Between the Ofsted inspection of 1994 and the subsequent one of 1999, the size of the school and the number of pupils eligible for free school meals rose significantly. There is not a large turnover of students but there is a 'passing population'. Pennywell takes students from five main feeder primary schools.

Prior to the present Head coming into post, Pennywell had had the same Head for 15 years: David Wilkinson, who led the school into the OCTET project but had to retire due to ill-health halfway through the summer term of 2001–02, almost one year after the project officially began.

When the OCTET project began, the school was ready for change. The Ofsted inspection report of 1999 described the school as low attaining but with satisfactory and good teaching. The RLS centre was opened in 2002 and the school was already spending significantly on ICT with a large-scale data projector in the hall, continuous video in the foyer and the RLS centre being used extensively during lessons, school breaks and outside school hours.

The new Head, Pat Pattison, joined Pennywell School in June 2002 following a positive Ofsted report that highlighted strong leadership and management plus good standards of teaching and behaviour. There were points for development highlighted but the inspection report was generally positive. However, compared to national standards of attainment, both at Key Stage 3 and at Key Stage 4, performance at the school was very low. This made the situation particularly complex because on the one hand teaching and learning was seen as satisfactory or good, but on the other attainment at the school was well below national average and lower than that achieved in neighbourhood schools. In the past decade performance has steadily improved. In 2002 attainment went to 17% from 13% in the previous year and in 2003 the school achieved 21%. For the last few years there has been a big push at Key Stage 3, both looking strategically at the quality of teaching and tactically at about how to boost the results.

The school serves a large white working-class estate with high unemployment. As the Head describes:

> There are at the moment 400 unoccupied houses that have been boarded up and some have been fire-bombed, some are just abandoned. Sunderland Housing are in the process of knocking down houses. There are, I think, 800 houses that are going to be knocked down and 600 rebuilt so that they

are lower density. The houses are very close packed and there is no green about this area; it is high density council house or ex-council houses and the place looks very dispiriting. When you see the young people out at the weekend, they are playing on the roofs of the broken down houses. We can't give them green in school but we can try to make up for this by giving them a good educational experience in the wider sense.

The Head is keen to make sure that the curriculum serves 'the needs of everybody' and therefore did not only focus on the 'A–C pupils'. Parents on the whole tended to be supportive of the school. The Head notes that some parents are supportive:

> but not able to have an influence on their children. Of course things that happen out on the estate at weekends and between families comes back into school and there can be problems that run on in school. We are then trying to manage situations that are not actually anything to do with us, but we try to do our best to get the families sorted and talking. The area is in the worst 5% of deprivation in the country. Our exam results are improving but we're at the top of all the indicators for deprivation and at the bottom of all the indicators for attainment.

The school's reputation over the years has been very mixed. In some quarters of the community there was a lot of affection for the school because of the immense amount of socially inclusive work the school does. However, with the introduction of league tables the school was judged differently as it was located so close to the bottom. As the Head outlines:

> If you have league tables, people make assumptions – if you're at the bottom of the league table you're not a good school. Then people come in and are very surprised by the amount of things going on and yes we do have very challenging youngsters here, and yes it is hard to work here but there's a lot of positives which I think the introduction of league tables ignores.

However, it was clear that the school was 'massively under performing'. Attendance remains poor at 86 per cent and for 'some youngsters obviously it's much worse than the average'. The Head notes:

> We have some very long-term absentees that we're working really hard to try and get in, but as they've not attended since primary it's hard to get them back in. There is a high, high proportion of children living in a family experiencing turbulence.

Initial stages

The school joined the OCTET project on the grounds that their attainment was low and the project offered an opportunity to look at other ways of raising attainment. The OCTET project also offered extra funding which was felt to be particularly valuable to the school. The project was presented as a way of rewarding and retaining staff. They were told that there would be incentives for teachers to stay in school and that there would be training and opportunities for extending the staff expertise as part of the project. Consequently staff were initially enthusiastic about the project and agreed to participate.

As noted earlier, the current Head was appointed midway through the project and found the initial introduction to the project complex and potentially confusing: 'I remember saying, "I don't see in what way it's a project". I could see that there'd been money put into the school, but it didn't seem cohesive as a project.'

The SIG had been selected by the previous Head and were also finding their way. The group that was operating within the school lacked adequate direction and in the first year failed to have a significant impact on school development. With some subsequent reconfiguration of the SIG and stronger guidance from the Head, the group began to operate more effectively.

> The SIG I feel is just now beginning to get off the ground, just as the project comes to an end. The SIG offers the potential for innovation linked into the main school developments. It's taken us a while but we've got there, and we can live with that.

The school found it difficult to manage some aspects of the SIG work. For example, the issue of cover caused major problems for the school at various times. 'The school is unsettled when there are so many people out. That has been an issue, but the SIG group has enjoyed the training.' In addition, the school lost SIG members to other schools who viewed their new skills as highly desirable. This was been seen as both unfortunate and inevitable by the senior management team. It became clear that as teachers gained more expertise from the OCTET project they were more likely to be targeted by other schools. The Head recognized that she didn't 'dig hard enough' into what other schools were doing with their SIGs, and how their SIGs were running. The school also invested heavily in interactive whiteboards and has seen major benefits from their introduction and usage.

> I'm not saying they're a panacea and they're the only way to teach, but they are another tool; they do make teaching look more twenty-first century for youngsters. The use of whiteboards has had an impact I think on the quality of teaching and learning.

In addition, the school invested in CAT testing as a way of being able to use data to identify teaching and learning needs. This was seen as an important and necessary investment that has now started to pay dividends.

> The school didn't use CAT testing before I came and we now do. We've got two years of youngsters with CAT data, and we are having INSET using SIG and other people on how to use the quadrants for learning styles.

The initial phase of the project focused upon changing the curriculum. When the new Head arrived at Pennywell School it was clear that there was a purely academic curriculum operating. In 2002, 83 per cent of pupils achieved no A*–C GCSE grades. Consequently, the Head introduced a new curriculum that focused upon vocational preparation and training. A vocational curriculum was introduced for Year 10 in the form of a new ICT course which was subsequently refined for Year 9. These changes meant that pupils had the option of vocational courses as well as the more academic subjects. Subsequently, the curriculum Deputy Head has been working on different pathways so pupils have the option to undertake a mixture of vocational and academic courses. In addition, the school is currently working with four other Sunderland South schools to create a sixth form and that will take the school forward again. As the Head summarizes:

> So yes, one of the things I have done is look at the curriculum with the banner of everyone matters, saying 'how does our curriculum fit?' And let's focus on all the children, not just the ones who are good, and able to get GCSEs.

HMI visits also proved to be an important component in the school's success. With a changed curriculum, the school inevitably changed aspects of its teaching: therefore, external scrutiny and feedback was considered to be particularly helpful:

The HMI has also got to know Pennywell and got to know what we're good at and what we're not so good at and been able to push us or nudge us in directions and keep us on our toes. I'm sure the staff would hate me for saying this because inspection twice a year is not what staff want, but I actually found that sharp HMI look at the place very useful, as did the rest of the leadership team and we trusted his judgement. We respected his judgement and I'm not saying we looked forward to his visits! But we always found them a very useful experience.

Many of the Pennywell visits occurred at critical times in the school's development and assisted the school in moving in the right direction and in becoming more self-evaluative. The leadership group changed the way they looked at teaching and learning in the school. Now a mini-inspection of departments is conducted regularly so that pressure is kept on improving teaching further. The leadership team currently observes every member of staff and provides feedback on teaching that is intended to be supportive and formative.

Impact

The school exam results are improving and there is a feeling in the school that the academic reputation of the school is also improving. In addition, the school has now met its floor targets which the Head acknowledges is 'a massive success'. She says: 'Being a leader in a school facing challenging circumstances means finding a balance between having time to do the strategic thinking, and being on the ground.'

The increase in the size of the leadership team has also meant stronger line management of staff. The leadership group meets weekly with each of the heads of department to achieve greater consistency in teaching throughout departments. Particular issues within departments are taken up in those meetings which have subsequently had a positive impact on quality of teaching and learning.

> I think one of the saddest things is that when Rob, the Deputy Head, and I came in last summer we felt sick for about a week before the results came in. The floor targets are so important. Initially the A–C pass rate came in at 19%. Then suddenly we were on 21% so there was a delayed frisson of pleasure and that's what the focus on those floor targets does to you. You forget about all the other things that you're doing and the fabulous music that we've produced, the school plays we've produced, the work on social

inclusion, the work schemes, the placements, the curriculum changes and you just focus in on this five A to Cs and your Key Stage 3 results.

Despite the improved exam results, the Head currently feels that the full impact of the OCTET project will not be felt for several years. She notes:

> One of the problems with projects like this that everybody expects results as it's happening and as it's ending, to be able to evaluate the effects, and you know, if you're working with a class of Year 7s in a school when a three-year project starts, you're not even going to have any results from them and if things you have embedded are having effect, the effects will be rolling on for years from now. I don't think it's yet possible to say what the overall effects of the project are because it's too soon.

The Head considers that some of the new teaching methods will be embedded in the long term but that some aspects of the OCTET project are not sustainable because of the removal of the extra resource. She is clear, however, that the SIG will remain and that the focus on teaching and learning will be maintained. It is the 'attention to teaching and learning' that the Head feels has made the biggest difference in terms of classroom performance:

> More or less everything we do is focusing on quality of teaching and learning, and I'm not saying it wasn't before, but I think I have sharpened the focus on that and I've probably in some cases made life for some staff more uncomfortable. And we've continued to try and work on behaviour for learning. So I would say focusing down on teaching and learning; slimming down planning so that it is focusing down on teaching and learning, has been our priority.

In addition to improved results, the school now enjoys a better reputation within the community. The Head notes:

> I do hear reports and governors hear reports that the perception of the school in the community is continuing to rise. It was rising – I'm not saying that's down to me, but it was rising and I think it is continuing to rise in the community.

The Head feels that the improved perception of the school is shared by pupils who have witnessed a change both in their classrooms and in the type of teaching they've experienced. Classrooms have been transformed through the introduction of interactive whiteboards and access to ICT. Staff perceptions and expectations have also changed for the better as they experience more positive responses from pupils to learning. Morale has risen and there are more teachers applying to work in the school. As the Head explains: 'People who do apply for jobs at the school say they have read that, or have heard that, it is an improving school.'

The future direction for the school is one of improving staffing and a general enthusiasm and passion for wanting to make things better. The leadership team is committed to supporting teachers in becoming better teachers and to providing the mechanisms to allow this to happen. The Head notes that there will be a great deal of support for

> teachers who are doggedly determined to be better teachers and to make things better for young people. It is a real joy when you see teachers flying. We have a lot of teachers here who can fly, who can take pupils with them, and who work enormous hours, enormous hours and work at weekends and run Saturday clubs, take them away for residentials to give them experience other than school, run coursework weekends; just so many staff work so hard.

Reflections

The Head feels that the key strategy for the future is having good teachers in front of classes and a leadership team which supports each other, shares ideas and makes suggestions in an atmosphere which is supportive and non-critical. The Head feels that the school has shifted in the last year from being defensive to being absolutely open and self-reviewing. The school's self-review process is now strong and teachers are not ashamed of sharing what they are doing well with other teachers.

> Staff review is crucial not just at leadership level, but at middle management level and at staff room level – teaching staff, reviewing their work. This system of review now underpins school improvement at Pennywell.

The school is involved in Building Schools for the Future and a new building is therefore planned for 2007. The Head feels that this development will make a significant difference to the school and will transform the current environment from one that is aging and badly designed. The four tower blocks with narrow stairs make it difficult to manage the school physically; consequently the new building offers the prospect of a better managed school and will prove to be a major bonus for the neighbourhood.

Reflecting on the lessons learned from the project the Head feels that sequencing and pacing change has proved to be important. She notes:

> Having patience – not expecting everything to come at once. Not getting frustrated because impact isn't instant – but you need to see some impact to see that you've made a start. Resilience and having the confidence as a staff to try things and to say, 'No! That's not working; we're not going to carry on doing that.' And if somebody has an idea, saying, 'Yes we'll give it a go' and being flexible and balancing what you're doing developmentally with what you're maintaining and not trying to develop everything at once – because you … you can't! That's what I meant about patience, having to pace things.

The new building will provide staff with an opportunity to look at how pupil support is organized and to revisit the way teaching and learning are managed within the school. The Head feels it offers an important means of reviewing all aspects of school functioning and ways of working.

7 Phoenix High School

Context and background

Phoenix High School is an 11–16 mixed city comprehensive in Shepherd's Bush, with 754 students on roll in 2003. The school is gaining in popularity: the roll has increased steadily in recent years. The school serves a high-density housing area in Shepherd's Bush and is within Hammersmith and Fulham LEA. The area is a volatile one due to the constant turnover of the population and this produces pockets of improvement and decline in the neighbourhood, described by one community worker as having the overall effect of 'a zero sum game'.

Phoenix High School opened in April 1995 as a 'fresh start' school, following the closure of the previous school in the site. The present Head William Atkinson was appointed as the new school opened. Prior to that, the school was called The Hammersmith School. The school was placed in special measures in 1994 and it was identified in the *Mail on Sunday* as the worst school in Britain. It came out of special measures and moved into serious weakness in 1997. The school has always had a very poor reputation and there was great difficulty in attracting and recruiting staff of the appropriate calibre. In addition there was a very challenging population, where youngsters had very poor prior attainment. Many of the able youngsters in the area either went or were sent to the high performing girl and boys' school locally and also to schools out of borough in Richmond, Wandsworth and Hounslow. The school population typically has 60% of pupils starting secondary school who read two years below their chronological age.

Like other schools in disadvantaged areas in London, there have been increasing difficulties with resourcing and staffing. To meet the needs of students in the areas of poverty in the capital city, a wide range of community resources are necessary in the school. Particular 'London issues' like the steeply rising costs of housing in London have made it more and more difficult to recruit long-term staff. In the year 2000, the school was feeling the brunt of the recruitment and retention crisis. The school has a significant number of refugee youngsters which contributes to a very high level of pupil mobility. Many of the youngsters are re-housed:

Some after a term, some two terms, a year, and when they're re-housed they leave the school and in so doing create vacancies which are then filled by other transient youngsters. In addition, about 80% of pupils come from one-parent families which generally provide loving and stable homes. However, in a minority of cases pressures prove too great for the single parent with the result that the pupil is moved around amongst the extended network both inside and outside of the local area, which results in the children in question moving schools on a regular basis. Also, historically, we've attracted a disproportionate number of excluded school youngsters, who continue to present inappropriately and end up excluded for a second or third time.

In short, these features contribute to a very high level of mobility – approximately 30 per cent plus in any given year, which sets up tremendous challenges for the school.

At the beginning of the OCTET project approximately a third of the staff in the school were supply teachers, or teachers on temporary contract. As the Head notes, there was a time in 2001 when the school

had run out of teachers, run out of supply teachers with the result that the senior team and I had to look after between four and nine classes each period each day for a period of about six weeks in the school dining hall. Some youngsters would spend up to three hours out of five hours outside of their normal lessons. This appalling state of affairs placed the school and everyone connected with it under considerable pressure. I was aware that a number of schools in different parts of the country had taken the difficult decision, in the face of chronic staff shortages, to send classes home.

The Head reflects, 'The judgement I made at that time, and on reflection it was the right judgement, was that the risks to the students were far greater out of school than inside.' However, this strategy was of concern for a large number of parents, who felt, rightly, that their children were being shortchanged by the school, and for students, who deeply resented the disruption to their education.

The resulting crisis tested the institution to its core. Matters were not helped by the arrival halfway through the term of a brown envelope announcing Ofsted's intention to inspect the school during the second week in January. Clearly this was a demoralizing period in the school's history which threatened to undermine and put in reverse the hard won achievements of the previous five years.

This was a very, very trying period for the staff especially for the permanent teachers, who were coming to school every day and not only had to carry their burden of the work, but also support and compensate for the temporary and non-existent colleagues. They were the staff getting the backlash from the children. They had to undo much of the negative experience that the youngsters had picked up in the previous hour/two hours.

It was also the case that the school had to dis-apply certain parts of the National Curriculum, e.g. modern foreign languages where it simply could not recruit.

The situation today at the school is much better in that staffing has improved, although the challenges in this area cannot be under-estimated. As the Head notes:

The level of challenge in my previous two headships, although tough, was nothing compared with life at Phoenix. I always had the staff needed. Even though you might only have two or three people to choose from at a short-listing, you always made an appointment, and when you didn't it was always possible to employ a good supply teacher to cover pending a re-advertisement. The use of a supply teacher in these circumstances made little or no impact because all the other people around them were good or stable people and the children were used to stable teachers so their patterns of behaviour were also fairly consistent. In this school you have dramatic changes from teacher to teacher.

In May 2003, when the school was removed from serious weaknesses, the percentage of lessons judged to be very good or excellent had fallen to somewhere in the region of 11 per cent; however the percentage of lessons judged to be satisfactory or better had increased to 95 per cent. The quality of teaching was an issue for the school. The Head notes:

The fact that staff mobility is so high meant that many of the off-the shelf prescriptions for fixing schools are absolutely useless because they've not been modelled against schools with these dynamic features.

The May 2001 Ofsted report identified many good things about the school. It reflected the fact that Phoenix School is a school which 'cares deeply for its students. They are valued and supported well in developing their self-esteem and potential as learners'. The report notes that: 'Provision for students' moral and social development is very good, cultural provision very good'. It goes on: 'Procedures for monitoring and supporting pupils' personal development are very good, procedures for monitoring and improving attendance are very good, procedures for monitoring and promoting good behaviour, monitoring and eliminating oppressive behaviour are outstanding.' Despite the positive report, until recently, exam results have been unsatisfactory. However, the school has improved significantly from its lowest point of 5% A*–C grades to a current level of 60%, plus the percentage of five or more A*–Gs has risen to 98%.

The Head notes:

> One major influence on our results is our highly variable intake. When the ability drops significantly, or is better, then you're going to have variations in performance which to a large extent is beyond the school's control.

The school's five or more A*–C results before the OCTET project started was somewhere in the region of 11%. The reputation of the school had improved dramatically up to the year or so before the start of the project. While much of the success of the school in recent years cannot be attributed to OCTET, the Head feels that the project has generated a number of good things:

> The project has helped build the capacity of the institution to respond. Also, alongside the project was some support from the neighbourhood regeneration which brought into the school health visitors, a school councillor on a full-time basis. A parent–student advocate, a full-time language–speech and language therapist working within the school. So that project gave us a number of practical things that we needed to actually support what was going on, alongside our own development as well as the support coming through the OCTET project.

Initial phase

Initial expectations of the OCTET project were founded on the fact that it would provide assistance to the work that the school was already undertaking and would help generate additional capacity. The development of a SIG was welcome because there had been a similar group previously which provided a framework for further development.

> The SIG has worked in a way that has supported the developments that we'd had in place in any event, and I think the support that the SIG's

had through the project has made that a more effective mechanism for support and development. The SIG was one of a number of important initiatives that over the last four or five years has supported the school's development.

The other significant development from within the OCTET project was the use of data:

> I think the project has really assisted us and moved us along the road in terms of using data to support learning and helping us to better manipulate the data, understand the data and link it to learning. The other tremendous gain from the project has been the introduction of whiteboard technology. Initially the catalyst was the project. I think creating the whiteboards policy within the school has been very beneficial in supporting a number of teachers and we now recognize that this is a very important tool when properly used.

Another positive aspect of the programme which was well received was the literacy work. The school had a good primary trained teacher

> who's been enthusiastic about it, and as a consequence achieved excellent results. However, where we've had to train secondary teachers without a deep background and understanding of how children learn to read and have the confidence to modify what's on offer, to bespoke it for the children, then it's not worked as well. But the principles are very good and I hope to continue this work beyond the project. So those are the major gains I see that have flowed from the project, and basically in terms of the expectations I had for the project, it's met those expectations.

Initially the Head was very concerned that the project was trying to force certain initiatives that did not fit into the school's development planning. However, through negotiation and watching the project unfold, the Head has become more convinced of its merits. In terms of successes, one clear example was that of whiteboard technology, as was mentioned above. Initially this development was received with some scepticism, but once the basic technology was mastered, and then applied, it then meant that those benefits were more readily shared.

The other initiative, also mentioned above, that made a difference to the school was the Literacy Programme: 'It's fantastic because it really just opens up the possibility that children can learn, it affects their confidence. So that's been a great gain.' The other area of the project identified as having a positive effect upon the school was the SIG, as mentioned above.

The SIG has actually allowed staff to take more responsibility for their development – initiatives are not just coming from the senior management leadership team within the school, but it's coming critically from staff who are drawn from across the school and so the training that's been put on for example, has been devised by the SIG. It has been provided by the SIG substantially and it's been joined up – not just discrete one-off experiences.

The SIG at the school consists of nine people including the Head, unlike other SIGs in the project. The reason for this, the Head suggests, is the fact that group doesn't have to broker things with the Head, who is fully aware of the developmental issues and plans.

It was very important for me to be part of the process, because I did not want to undermine nor frustrate the people who were giving up their time to do this work. So I'm part of it.

There is a learning support assistant in the group, a newly qualified teacher plus an overseas teacher and several middle managers. The SIG goes right across the school and it contains people with different experiences, different curriculum areas, but as the Head notes, 'All people who are interested in the school improvement and playing a part in that.'

Impact

The term 'exceptionally challenging circumstances' the Head feels is both an apt and possibly understated description of the day-to-day challenges staff face at Phoenix School. Yet, teachers maintain a resilience and optimism that young people can still learn and that the school can go on improving. But the Head feels that the continuing rise in student performance tells only part of the story

because education excellence is measured not by exam results or by value added, but by lived values. It is measured by the hope given to young people that there is something better than their prior experience and that learning is for life.

The Head continues to play a very active 'hands on' role in the daily life of the school. His vision and values are apparent in his everyday actions.

I know a lot because I'm out of this office, I'm out there. I know what's going on in the classrooms, I cover lessons. I meet the heads of faculties individually; I meet the teachers who are teaching Year 9 and Year 11, setting their targets for them, reviewing their performance. This is a very hands-on kind of organization where things all the time go wrong so one needs to be in tune, in touch to try and catch it before it goes wrong, or make a response as it goes wrong because if you don't do that it gathers momentum and it's so easy to undermine. So you just need to keep your finger on the pulse all of the time!

Also the Head feels that the school makes an important contribution to the community and needs to be actively seen by the community: 'Local people need to see us, and to feel that we're taking responsibility.'

Looking back on the OCTET project, the Head feels that the school would not be 'as far down the road' with the use of data quadrants and the CAT analysis without the project because 'I don't think we would ever have had the momentum.' The Head feels that the biggest single thing that's going to transform the school over the next few years is consistent attention to how pupils learn best. Within the school OCTET has played a role but not the most important role in securing improvement. The Head confirms that the project has been very helpful but that other developments have made more of an impact on schools.

> Genuinely I can say it's been an important project that has contributed to the evolution of this school at various critical points in terms of certain initiatives and developments which have actually taken place and I'm sure that without the OCTET initiative our progress in some of those areas would have been slower.

Considering the other schools in the OCTET project, the Head notes that they share a number of important elements. Firstly, they share highly resilient staff 'because in these kinds of schools things go wrong all the time'. Second, it is likely that all OCTET schools have difficulty recruiting the best and retaining the best staff, 'Although many excellent staff work in these schools, simply because of the level of challenge and in a situation of shortage teacher shortage then there's an incentive for teachers to work in easier schools and be paid the same – they still work very hard of course – but have a much easier life.' Third, they share the challenge to really engage young people and make them feel powerful as learners. 'I think that's got to be universal because when you have lower prior attainment it often means that self-esteem is low and without good self-esteem you see yourself as more likely to fail than succeed, therefore you don't commit or engage, you find alternative things to do.'

Reflections

The Head's priorities for the school in the future focus upon high quality teaching and learning and high expectations. The Head feels that teachers need to set high expectations which are maintained irrespective of the context, 'irrespective of what the kids are giving you back'. An integral part of maximising the performance of young people the Head suggests must be 'the very best teaching we can produce to support the potential learner to achieve. So there is no choice about that; that's the way it's got to be otherwise you end up colluding with your circumstances, and you've got to buck your circumstances; you're working against that'. The main priority for the school is to be an effective school for young people and to be a school that makes a difference in their lives; a school that transforms their life chances.

> That's been the goal from day one. And to do that we need to support them
> in the classroom very much in the way we've talked about, but crucially we
> must be supporting them outside of the school. This school is about more
> than getting good exam results. It is fundamentally about growing young
> people which involves exposure to a range of education opportunities and
> challenges outside of the classroom as well as inside.

The ways the school is aiming to meet these aspirations include peer mentoring systems, a high achievers club, the school council, junior and senior prefects and many other methods of motivating and rewarding young people.

The Head has very high expectations for the school, very high expectations of the teachers, very high expectations of the students, very high expectations of their parents. He notes:

> one mustn't lose sight of that and one of the things that has always
> informed my own thinking is the absolute need to guard against any form
> of complacency or any form of activity or thinking that could amount to
> collusion with low expectations.

The aim is to keep progress under review to check the most effective measures are in place, how well they work and 'if they're not there, to modify accordingly'.

8   Ridings School

Context and background

The Ridings School is a mixed non-selective 11–16 comprehensive with 735 students on roll in 2003–04. The school was created in 1995 by the amalgamation of two secondary modern schools. It is one of seven secondary schools in Halifax, which include two selective grammar schools, two selective faith schools and two high schools. Three of the four selective schools lie within two miles of The Ridings School. The school is situated in the Ovenden ward of Calderdale where 95 per cent of the pupils attending walk to school from Ovenden and the adjoining wards of Mixenden and St John's.

When The Ridings School was formed in January 1995, the school was led by a newly appointed head, who left 'with immediate effect' in October 1996. This resignation triggered an emergency Ofsted inspection and the LEA appointed two headteachers to lead the school in November 1996, one of whom is the current Head, Anna White. In October 1996 The Ridings was placed in 'special measures' and had to deal with negative international press coverage of the first so-called 'failing school' in England. Pupils, parents, teachers and the whole community felt utterly demoralized. Anna White assumed sole responsibility for the school in September 1997. At this stage she was able to begin appointing a number of key staff, including a leadership team. The school came out of special measures in October 1998.

The majority of pupils have EBD needs, and within the school approximately 30 per cent of children are of average ability. Six per cent of pupils have statements and 42 per cent are on the Special Needs register. The majority of pupils come from households where unemployment is now in its third generation. In many cases the child may be the only person in a household getting up in the morning with a purpose. According to Social Services statistics for 1998, more than 30 per cent of children in three wards lived in families claiming income support. Halifax has suffered a major decline in employment over the last 20 years with the industrial recession of the 1970s and 1980s resulting in the closure of major engineering and textile factories. North Halifax is now considered to be part of the Leeds regional sub-economy and the new jobs are in the supply services, offices and high technology. Industries are not always seen as accessible or attractive to the local communities. Between 1997 and 2003 an average 22.6 per cent of the total Calderdale population were unemployed.

The school has made concerted efforts to reach the community and engage with parents, but this has proved difficult. The Head, Anna White, notes:

> I've got be realistic and perhaps I'm more realistic than I was eight years ago, but I think if we can change the perceptions of some of the cohort that we have in each year group into understanding that staying on at school post-16 and going away to university, or getting a career as opposed to a job, and then returning to give something back to the community, that's how it'll begin to change. But it's such a big job, it can't be the school on its own, it has to be the council, social services, the police. I think that at last we're beginning to work together.

Initial phase

The school accepted the offer to be part of the OCTET project because of the extra funding and the fact that the project was clearly aimed at improving teaching and learning. There was a real wish to see the school continue to improve, so the OCTET project offered a concrete way of trying new things and sharing good practice. The issue of HMI monitoring as part of the project was not seen a problem for the school as it had been subjected to regular HMI visits while in special measures. The Head notes: 'We just feel like we've been under the spotlight constantly since 1996 to be honest.'

There was a meeting in London for heads of schools in challenging circumstances in December 1998 that the Head attended. She reflected:

> Eight people who'd never met before, who didn't know anything about each other met in this room, we didn't know how we'd been selected, but basically we agreed to join because we could possibly get about a million pounds additional funding. Eight schools working together with some central money. It seemed too good not to say yes, so of course we signed up.

Apart from the financial incentive, 'which didn't actually amount to anything near a million!', the Head felt that expectations of the project were fully met. Despite being badly organized in the first year, once a project manager was appointed (Sue James), the project gained momentum and began to make headway. In the first year the school was able to appoint additional staff in the area of literacy and science. In the first few months of the project, however, the eight headteachers did not really meet.

> We didn't know anything about each other and we didn't for ages. We were never told anything about each other so we had to sort of say 'What's your school story and where are you?' and make some connections that way. Nobody gave us pen portraits ... we didn't even really know why we'd been chosen to start with, but we found out eventually that we'd all been selected because we'd had good Ofsted reports about management and leadership and that we had high percentages of students on free school meals and high numbers of students with special needs. But it became very clear to the eight of us that we were very different schools and that the Ofsted reports perhaps, didn't tell the full story, so we weren't eight schools in similar circumstance at all really.

Each of the eight schools was allowed to employ more staff, but in the first year of the project 'little else seemed to happen'. In the second year the staff development programme was launched and the SIGs from each of the schools were established. These groups were intended to be the catalysts for change and development both within schools and across the eight schools. After the first residential meeting, the SIG came back enthused 'and ready to take on new initiatives. At our school the SIG group deliver all in-service training and work with staff on teaching and learning issues'. The configuration of this group, however, has changed over the life of the project, as people have been promoted out of school. The Head feels that this is one of the down sides of the project: 'The fact that staff really do understand teaching and learning and the improvement agenda means we now have only two existing members in our SIG.'

The original SIG members were selected from teachers who were fully committed to professional development and who wanted to work across the school. The Head decided not to join the SIG as she wanted it to lead development and change from the middle rather than from the top down. 'I wanted them to know that they were driving innovation and that they had a clear say in the curriculum of the school and in what we did as a school on teaching and learning.' The

SIG attended all the training sessions provided by the OCTET and as a group were instrumental in disseminating and trailing new approaches with staff. The school had undertaken a lot of work on ICT prior to joining the project. They were already working to enhance their literacy and numeracy skills by using an open integrated learning programme. The school was also part of an Education Action Zone which put the majority of money into ICT so primary and secondary schools worked together. The OCTET project enabled the school to buy additional whiteboards which have subsequently had a big impact in classrooms. The school would like to purchase many more whiteboards.

The school had assessed Year 7 students using CAT for a long time and had used the data to look at both verbal and non-verbal scores. The Head notes: 'The opportunity to look at children's learning styles in relation to their scores was something that the project provided and was considered to be very valuable.' The teachers found the data fascinating and illuminating. As the Head notes:

> They got hooked into it. It has made a real difference and data is now talked about all the time. What it's meant is that the data that now goes out to staff is real data, it's not figures that they just say 'Oh yes'... they really are looking at it, we pour over it, our data is real and live and informs our planning and delivery.

Impact

The SIG proved to be a major success of the project. In addition the RML programme was well received and it was used with classes in Years 7, 8 and 9. These were classes that school felt would benefit from the programme. The Head reflected:

> We found very quickly that RML 2 was too difficult and we had to do RML 1 which was the programme for primary school, our students couldn't cope with RML 2. RML 1 was a success, you can see children gaining confidence and beginning to read with understanding as opposed to just recognizing words on a page.

The middle management training also was considered to be a success and the residential for middle managers was very well received.

The Head feels that being one of the eight proved to be a significant factor. The mutual support and the 'common ground' meant that the headteachers understood each other's needs and bonds with schools were formed. The additional external support from the DfES Project Manager was also considered to be vital. 'Having Sue James find out things for you and point you in the right direction or say "Yes of course you can", or "Have you tried this?" That's been great as well, absolutely superb.' The removal of these resources, however, is a matter of some concern. 'It seems stupid to give a school so much support and access to things and then take it away, if they do that now after three years then how do we maintain the momentum we have carefully built up?'

At the beginning of the project the Head saw her role as securing as many resources as possible while recognizing the danger of going into 'initiative overload'.

> There is a fine line with how much you can take on and in the past five or seven years we've been really heavily involved with an enormous number of initiatives. But again you can't let that suddenly stop either, you've got to keep a certain amount on to make sure that things are happening in the school.

Being the voice of the school and making sure it was heard and listened to was a prime role the Head played. The Head felt that it was important 'to keep banging the drum and saying "You're not listening. You really don't understand the difficulties we are facing".'

Within the school the recruitment of staff has proved to be more difficult than it was seven years ago. The OCTET project has also added to some of the retention difficulties as staff from the SIG are seen as very valuable assets to other schools.

> Every single member of staff who has applied for an external post has been promoted to the job that they've gone for because everybody knows that if they are successful here they will be successful anywhere! They're streets ahead in interviews because they're talking about preferred teaching and learning styles and CATs analysis and data management etc. – all topics we've worked on through the OCTET project.

The major achievements of the project have been the positive impact on attainment and the fact that 'the children feel better about education; they feel better about themselves; they want to stay on into the sixth form; we offer them a curriculum that suits their needs; we offer them a Post 16 curriculum that's going to give them something worthwhile'. The school is currently feeling positive about the future and staff are keen to continue their work on teaching and learning that started within the OCTET project. The last HMI monitoring report had a positive reception as it was supportive of the school and what it has achieved.

Reflections

Looking back on the project, the Head notes that RML was probably not an appropriate strategy to use with Year 9 students. Even so, the programme did have a positive effect upon their behaviour as pupils are 'slightly better behaved in class and listen to each other'. The continued emphasis for the school 'is not just on teaching styles, but how children learn'. The Head feels that the shift of focus on learning rather than teaching has been the biggest change in the school alongside the use of data to inform teaching.

> I think those have been the biggest changes that we've seen and I think staff see these as very positive things. In terms of parents, the Head feels that although parents would not know what the OCTET project was, they would think that the school has continued to grow and improve over the last eight years.

The Head feels that public perception of the school is still a barrier and notes that memories last a very long time. There is still an issue with student mobility because the school is in an economically poor and very socially deprived catchment area where families move in and move out quite frequently. The current rate is about 15 per cent turnover per year. As the Head notes:

> You don't really choose to come The Ridings; I'd love that to be the case and it seems disloyal of me to say that families don't, but I don't think you suddenly change schools in Year 9 and think I'll go to The Ridings, I've got a better chance of getting five A–Cs if I move. So pupils' mobility is a difficulty as are staff retention and recruitment – these are difficulties that schools like this share. I think my main barrier would probably still be a deep lack of understanding by the DfES of what it is like to work in a school like this year in year out.

The school constantly strives to improve its physical environment. 'We are well aware that the facilities that we have in school now are probably nicer than a lot of our children have at home.' The Head identifies that patience is important in a school context such as The Ridings and the endless willingness to 'try something else if one initiative fails'. The school intends to apply for Specialist College status.

> We've got all the money, we've got the sponsors, there's a will from the sponsors to help us get the status so the bid's going in again at the end of March. I didn't think we'd get it last time; this time I am more hopeful and I think we'll be hurt, emotionally hurt, if we don't succeed – we won't feel badly done to, but it'll just wound us and we'll have to lift ourselves up from it. It would be a really good thing for us to achieve Specialist Status.

The school is part of a soft federation which is providing another aspect to concentrate on and to be proud of. The school is also part of a Family Learning Initiative and is doing work with community champions to build stronger links between the community and the school. Other priorities for the school are to maintain 20% A*–C GCSE grades and to ensure the children in school feel proud of what they achieve. The school also aims to grow its sixth form and to provide a whole raft of courses to meet the needs of a diverse student population. In summary, the school's future priorities are: increasing the sixth form; increasing the community's involvement in school; and achieving the Specialist Arts School status. The school recognizes that it is probably one of the biggest employers in the community. 'While a lot of the teaching staff don't live locally, all our support staff do and many of our admin staff do and therefore the school aims to be more central to the community.'

In terms of advice to other schools the Head suggests that schools need to be in for

> the long haul. Don't for one minute believe that it's an 18-month turn around and then everything's hunk dory. I don't think any Heads ever did believe in Superheads, there was a belief in government wasn't there, that you turned schools round in 12 months? And there still are some heads who are shipped in to do that and then walk away. And, you know, we could all do that! But it's keeping it going that's hard. It's hard. Take risks. Be prepared to take risks. Be prepared to take the knockbacks as well as the glory. Accept responsibility for everything, but share the accolades of success with everyone!

The other piece of advice offered by the Head is:

> Listen to the children, listen to the parents. Work with the LEA, work with
> anybody who you think can help you and be prepared to have failures as
> well because if you're prepared to take chances and risks – you know – half
> of them won't work, but then there'll be lessons to learn from them along
> the way. Listen to your heart as well as your head.

9 St Albans School

Context and background

St Albans is a Church of England school. It is an inner-city school on a small site with limited sports and playing facilities and is the only secondary school within the Inner Ring Road in Birmingham. It is located in an area with a high density of population. The majority of the ward population (77.9 per cent) are from ethnic minorities and include a high proportion of people with few or no qualifications. The present Head David Gould took up his post in 1999, just before the OCTET project began. The school had had an Ofsted inspection in 1999 which praised the dedication of the staff and the effective leadership in the school and voiced concerns about the low attainment at Key Stage 4, the lack of language support and the lack of vocational courses at Key Stage 4.

The ethnic and cultural mix at the school shifts from year to year. There are on average 37 different first languages spoken by the students and at least 50 per cent of the students speak English as a second language. There is a large Muslim population in the area, some of whom send their children to a Church of England school because it is a religious school. More that 60 per cent of the students are eligible for free school meals. Officially 44.7 per cent of students have special educational needs (this is down from official figures of 64.7 per cent two years previously). There are 30 feeder primary schools, which means a fragmented intake into Year 7. Students from the most local primary school, Chandos, move on to a large number of different secondary schools, some of which are a distance away from St Albans. The school has a 10 per cent rate of absence for 2004 and this has been reduced from 11.9 per cent in 2003, 12.5 per cent in 2002 and 17.3 per cent in 2001. A significant number of students (265 in 2003) did not gain any GCSE/GNVQ qualifications.

The school currently has 430 students, whereas in 1991 there were only 250 students. The Head believes that the school is 'bursting at the seams' and that at an intake of 87 students each year it is a full as it can be. The school is in the poorest part of one of the ten most deprived wards in the country. It's a school that's always been vulnerable to threats of closure and has always successfully resisted because it is valued in the community as a Church of England school. The school is the only comprehensive school in the area and the only secondary school inside the middle ring road of the city, so as it is nearest to the city centre it is in a very special situation. The school has been particularly vulnerable because in successive years it has been near or at the bottom of the league tables. This has meant that HMI and Ofsted have always had concerns and scrutinized the school very carefully.

The school has an extremely high number of special needs pupils and 50 per cent of the students speak English as an additional language. The Head notes that

> many are new arrivals who come to the country speaking little or no English and many of them have come from places like the Yemen where they've got no education in their own language and no literacy in their own language so there's no conceptual basis on which to build, so it takes an awfully long time with those students to make them at all literate.

In terms of performance the value added at Key Stage 3 is low. In 2003 the value added at Key Stage 3 was 97.6 which is just above the bottom 5 per cent, but at Key Stage 4 it was 100.9. The most challenging aspect of the school is its low prior attainment on entry. It has the lowest profile of attainment of the eight schools in the project, which presents very particular challenges in terms of meeting the Government's floor targets. 'The children are not especially challenging, they're not very streetwise, they're very immature, they're kind of – a lot of them are very primary school-like.'

The average pupil turnover for the school is over 30 per cent and as the Head notes:

> there is always a danger that you could get, for various reasons, long term absence of staff or whatever, that you could get quite easily put in special measures by Ofsted or by an HMI visit and the knock-on effect of that in terms of recruitment and so on, could quite easily lead to a situation where you're under-staffed where therefore you get into a kind off downward spiral where you can't get out of special measures.

In 1996 the school had an Ofsted inspection which was reasonably successful but HMI looked at the data 18 months later and decided that the school had serious weaknesses. As a consequence, the school had an HMI visit, a monitoring visit, which resulted in the judgement of 'satisfactory progress'. In 1999 the school had its second Ofsted which found that 99 per cent of the teaching was satisfactory or better and that the school was well led and managed. At this time the headteacher retired and the current Head David Gould, took over. During this period the school had a huge influx of new and unsettled students – with a turnover of about 45 per cent in the 12 months that followed, which resulted in lots of challenges.

In December 2000 the Head received a personal invitation to attend a conference in London and at the end of that conference DfES representatives met with the headteachers of the eight OCTET schools and proposed the OCTET project. The OCTET project provided the school with significant sums of additional money, and the possibility of establishing a formative relationship with DfES over a period of a few years. The Head considered it to be a very good opportunity and in addition, thought it would potentially give the school 'protection from Ofsted and HMI for three or four years'. However, in practice this was not the case as HMI were involved in the project from the start and they visited the school regularly. Although a formative relationship was developed with schools they retained their usual way of working. The Head notes:

> they commented on the quality of teaching and learning and the quality of leadership and management and that was their first and primary focus on every visit so it was really quite challenging and as a result of it one of the schools did go into special measures and hasn't been able to participate very much in the project as a result of that.

One of the main reasons for joining the project was the extra resource generated for the school. The additional resource enabled the Head to secure two new appointments to the senior leadership team and both were new people from outside. They were permanent appointments, both at assistant headteacher level. So the school moved from a leadership team of just three with very little time for strategic leadership and management to a team of five with two very experienced teachers coming in from other schools in the city. This outside view was felt to be very important in such a close-knit, small school. The extra money also allowed the school to appoint new teachers, new non-teaching staff and support staff: 'We had basically good teachers, the people we brought in were good, we had the skills and the knowledge to do what we wanted to do but we didn't have the time and the energy.'

In addition, the school was given extra resource in the form of staff development. In particular, the training for middle managers, the SIG and developments in ICT have proved to be very positive.

> The project has been extremely positive for the school, particularly with regard to the SIG training, the middle management training and the general staff development that we've had. We used the Really Mastering Literacy programme which was commissioned particularly for the project and we've had the most success with that; that's been entirely positive for us. We trained six teachers; we had 100 children doing it in the first year, so basically half of Year 7 and half of Year 8 doing an hour a day on that programme. The teachers were very positive about it and the progress was good. We're continuing with that. It's a smaller cohort now because obviously the older ones have already been through it, but we've still got two groups in Year 7 and one in Year 8 and we're actually promoting that project in the education action zone as well.

The school has developed ICT because of the increased capacity that they have had through the OCTET project. There has been some good whiteboard training but because the school only has a small number of whiteboards, it has had a relatively focused impact, not a wide impact across the school.

> It's made us realize what is possible and what we want to achieve; it hasn't technically helped us to achieve it because their technical solutions have gone wrong but it has helped us to find our own way towards where we want to go.

Initial stages

It was anticipated that the OCTET project would provide the increased capacity to enable the school to be more stable. As the Head notes:

> You can't begin a process of school improvement if your foundations aren't secure. The increased capacity at senior leadership level and at middle management level, and the training that we've had, has made the biggest difference because it's impacted in all areas; everything that we've been trying to do.

In the initial stages people were invited to come forward to form the SIG. The Head notes:

They were mostly very good people, very good teachers, very ambitious and effective people and we took on board the recommendation that there should be a member of the senior leadership team involved and that was me but in practice I've not actually been involved, I've been kept well informed, but I felt it was better because they were confident so I just let them get on with it, Because I felt if I was there they kept turning to me. So there's ups and downs of having done that. There are problems as a result where I think the senior leadership team and the SIG are not as closely meshed as they might otherwise have been and we need to work on that.

Throughout the OCTET process the involvement of HMI proved to be critical. There was a preliminary visit and subsequently four visits by the link HMI attached to the project. In the second visit the school felt that it really 'got to grips' with the fact that there were big problems in the leadership of two important curriculum areas. The leaders of these subjects had been in post since 1973 and the quality of teaching needed urgent attention. The clear implication to the governors and the LEA was that if the school didn't address this problem there was a real possibility of being put into special measures. Consequently, the Head put the two assistant headteachers appointed through the project in charge of one of these subject areas and promoted the second in department to take over as leader of the other.

So a lot of progress has been made in those areas, and HMI have been back twice since to confirm that. HMI's involvement has actually helped to put pressure on these people and bring about change more quickly.

The main benefit of the OCTET project to the school has been its contribution to increasing capacity. The school has agreed developmental priorities and has worked to train teachers to becoming more able practitioners. The Head acknowledges, however, that the community relationship is the most difficult aspect to change.

The community is the hardest bit because we have some loyal clients who've been sending their children for years and one of the things ... and they had low expectations really ... and they thought the school was safe. I don't just mean physically safe, I mean safe in colloquial way, he's safe, that teacher's safe because he's not very strict! He lets me just chill out. So we've become much more challenging in terms of requirements for school uniform and that kind of stuff and demanding that the parents come to consultation events and making high demands about behaviour and attitudes and making demands on their parents if their children don't behave the way we need them to and all that kind of stuff. That gradually has an effect and in terms of the number of parents that we actually get in to speak to, that has had a big effect so that whereas we typically only got about 20 per cent of parents attending consultation events, we've got an average of up to about 60 per cent now.

In the past the school only contacted parents when there was a problem with a child and the parents could be very angry and upset; it wasn't very positive. But now the school says to parents we need your cooperation because we want your child to stay at school to catch up with its course work. This has proved to be very positively received and parents have been then they're entirely supportive.

The attendance at out-of-hours learning and holiday schools is also very good. The school feels that it is moving in the right direction; the children are better dressed, their behaviour is better, their attendance is better. What is really important to the school is that every child achieves their potential and that the school provides a safe and secure learning environment.

The Head recognizes, however, that because of external circumstances such as poverty and associated socio-economic factors, a significant proportion, of students will achieve no external qualifications. Part of the reason for this resides in the home background factors. In short, it is difficult for the school to get a really good attendance because of things that happen in the home that affect progress.

> We have a vast number of child protection issues, almost daily referrals to social services, there's abuse of various kinds and neglect. There are drug issues obviously – there is crime – all these things impact on attainment and then aspirations. But all I can say is that we're making progress but obviously there needs to be a recognition of the cost and impact of poverty and until the government gives a proper ongoing commitment to fund schools in deprived areas much more than in other schools ... a project like this, successful as it has been, it has been successful because of the increased capacity.

Impact

The Head feels that the OCTET project has contributed to capacity building for improvement. Its unrelenting focus on teaching and learning the things we would be doing is gradually reducing the turnover. Currently we've still got a 30 per cent turnover.

The OCTET project enabled the school to learn through collaboration by networking with other schools. The school found it very valuable working with OCTET schools 'because they face similar challenges, and so things that were done in the other schools I have learned from, and there have been practices that we've adopted'. For example, the school adopted an assessment system from Whitefield School and now assess all the students every term to a third of a National Curriculum level. There is also a termly target setting review day where the normal timetable is abandoned and parent, teachers and pupils get together to review progress.

> It's one of the things that's helped us to get parents in because we said you only come to school that day for 15 minutes, but you bring a parent, we have a good 15-minute talk through about the progress you're making and what you need to do to get better in the future.

Reflections

OCTET has provided a range of opportunities for St Albans in addition to sharing good practice. The training of staff, developing teams of people and the focus upon the teaching and learning have all been particularly influential and a powerful means of change at the school. In the past the school had been involved in 'too many different initiatives' and 'had no time to stop and think at all'. In contrast, the OCTET project did provide the time to plan, review and reflect. The school has been able to look at its strategic objectives and to ensure that various initiatives and developments in support of these objectives were properly coordinated.

The success of the OCTET project was its concentration upon a small number of absolutely key strategic objectives. To make this work the Head had to ensure that everyone in the organization was equally focused on these priorities.

> You have to have a very robust process that makes you absolutely certain that those are the right things that you are pursuing. It was quite obvious in these circumstances that we had to raise expectations, that we had to work more closely with parents and that we had to focus on the basic skills as

has been impacted as well as being well informed by data. It also mea
building the processes within the school to support professional dialog
and learning. The SIG has been instrumental in driving change at t
school and leading improvement. As the Head notes:

> The whole point was that this was going to be not bottom up change, but
> through a group that was representing the whole school and that would be
> able to take things forward.

The issues facing the school, however, were: how do you bring the scho
improvement group into the normal structures of the school? How do yo
review the structures of the school to recognize the fact that you've no
got an SIG driving things forward? These were addressed by improvin
communication between the senior leadership team and the SIG.

The school has also been seeking to improve the environment and t
improve facilities to attract pupils from more affluent homes. The Hea
notes:

> The parents that are more ambitious for their children think that if they
> send them further out of the inner city, they will get to a better school and
> a better education. It's not actually true as it happens, but that's what they
> think – that's what happens. So that's why we have ludicrous numbers of
> kids with special needs coming in, you know, in the past it's been up to
> 83 per cent.

The Head is confident that a continued level of funding will allow
the school to improve in all areas. There is a recognition that a mor
balanced intake would allow the school, in time, to achieve 30 or 4(
per cent five A*–C grades. As the only Church of England school withir
the city, the school wants to serve its immediate community as well a
attracting more able pupils who want a church school. The logic of th
school's partnership with St Peter's School in Wolverhampton is to buil
on the shared religious foundation and, by doing so, to raise expecta
tions. The Head wants to develop the site, improve the buildings, expan
the numbers and improve the results and continue to raise expectation;
He feels that the school has been doing this but that much more coul
be done.

> I believe we're making progress in that direction, I believe OCTET has
> helped but a school with an annual turnover of more than 12 per cent of
> students finds it almost impossible to maintain school improvement. One of

soon as possible that the students needed in order to access the secondary curriculum and to try and cut through the rest of the stuff and only use it to support those few objectives – to make sure that everybody is signed up to those but then you've got to work on the people and giving the people the capacity to take those things forward.

10 Whitefield School

Context and background

Whitefield School is a county comprehensive with specialized Sports School status located in the Outer Borough of Barnet. It is a mixed 11–18 school with approximately 800 students on roll. It is situated in Golders Green ward, a multi-ethnic area. Statistics show unemployment running at about the national average and crime statistics broadly in line with those elsewhere in England and Wales. Of the ward, 39.2 per cent live in flats, more than twice the national average, and a much higher proportion (25.5 per cent) than average live in privately rented accommodation. There is no natural catchment area for the school and some pupils come from as far as ten miles away. This makes marketing the school difficult as it is not clear which parents should be targeted.

Whitefield is a school with a high proportion of ethnic minority pupils (between 60 and 80 per cent over the last five years) and particular ethnicities which shift over time. The number of pupils with EAL has varied between 49 and 59 per cent over the last five years with currently 78 languages represented; and the number of asylum seekers and refugees is high. The large number of pupils from various different ethnic groups is seen as a strength of the school because 'everyone is in a minority group' and there is no overall dominant culture in the school. However, the school is constantly challenged to target its various initiatives to a shifting intake and to properly meet the diverse set of needs that this shifting intake presents. The present make-up of the school is still skewed towards the bottom end of the academic attainment range in that a large proportion of its pupils have special educational needs and low literacy levels; there has been a range of 33 per cent to 45 per cent special educational needs over the last five years with around 5 per cent statemented.

The main issue for the school is movement of students both in and out of the school. Mobility is still about 18 per cent annually though it has been as high as 20 per cent per term. These casual admissions can be students new to the country and sometimes new to schooling (e.g. asylum seekers and refugees) and many may well move again shortly after arriving in the school. At the beginning of the OCTET project, the headteacher's view was that more middle-class parents were often reluctant to 'risk' the school.

The student data would indicate about 50 per cent on free school meals, and that between 40 and 50 per cent had English as a second language. Basically all of the major indicators of disadvantage fall around the 50 per cent mark and have not really changed over the last decade. A large number of pupils at the school are new to the country, so overall the school has a fair amount of disadvantage. However, the school scores relatively highly in terms of aspiration taking into account YELIS data. The Head notes: 'Sometimes what you've got is quite bright students that don't have prior attainment levels or have very low prior attainment levels not to do with their ability but to do with their EALness.'

The school has had two full Ofsteds, one in 1996 and the other in 1999, both of which were good. The 1999 report indicated lots of progress and improvement. PANDA data is indicating small levels of improvement in terms of comparisons with like schools. The school is in a family of London Challenge schools that 'are not too different from where we are. But I think this is a better organised school than many of those and I think Whitefield runs more smoothly and much more harmoniously.' The Head feels that insufficient weight is given to the disadvantage the school faces and what is being achieved.

> The school now looks like a good learning environment but I think people then ask, 'Well if it's a good learning environment, why aren't the students performing better?' and the answer is, actually they are performing better. When Whitefield wasn't a good learning environment we were at 11 per cent, so it's a massively better learning environment. There is a Catch 22, the better you make one, then the more people expect of you and there comes a limit to how much you can actually do in terms of that improvement without a fundamental change of cohort.

The school became a Sports College just over five years ago and the Head feels that this was important and changed the attitudes of many pupils towards the school for the better.

> We're probably at the stage where some parents are still saying, 'I wouldn't consider Whitefield for my child'. But we've got a large number of parents who are saying, 'Well why not?' Almost 100 per cent of the parents say that they'd send their child here.

Initial phase

The initial attraction of the OCTET project was the extra resources.

> That's almost number 1, 2 and 3. The other reasons were ... it sounded
> quite interesting, it sounded quite fun actually to be involved, it sounded
> like there was someone who genuinely wanted to understand what schools
> in very, very challenging circumstances were like and make some difference
> to them and support them in improving. And certainly for me it was
> because I needed some money to be able to do some of the things that I
> wanted to do. Essentially to give teachers time to organize quality planning
> and teaching.

The school was originally promised £330,000 a year which dropped to
£150,000. The other reason for joining the project was OCTET project
was because it was seen as fairly high profile and was considered to be a
high status project.

> It gave us a quality feel about what we were doing and I think did provide
> a large resource to make us move on a little bit faster than possibly we
> would have done. Certainly it wasn't in a different direction to the one we
> were going.

The OCTET project was seen as offering some solutions to problems
the school was facing and the use of data was considered an important
dimension that the school wanted to address. The Head feels that the
OCTET project also allowed the school to take a more external look at
itself: 'I think being part of the OCTET project has probably given us
confidence in our ability to say "look we are actually fine".' The culture
that has been developed in the school over the last probably three or
four years has been helped very significantly by being part of the OCTET
project. The Head feels the reasons for this shift in culture has been the
interaction with other heads and the SIG interaction with staff. The
school has now SIG 2 and SIG 3 planned, that is, more groups of staff
who are operating in the same way. One group is looking at accelerated
learning, the other will focus on the use of technology in learning.

Initially the Head was apprehensive about joining the group of eight
schools.

> I didn't really want to be with the Ridings and Phoenix, they sounded like
> scary places, but actually not scary at all. As usual, not like their reputation

and they've been fine. In fact The Ridings is probably the school in terms of senior management who we link to most closely although their student profile is very different. The Phoenix is a school that we relate to most closely in terms of student profile.

The fact that the project was premised on collaboration rather than competition between the schools was viewed as a positive aspect. This meant that the heads were able to have an honest discussion and to share concerns and problems openly.

The school has been quite fortunate in terms of staff changes as these have been lower than other schools in the project. This has helped the permeation of the project into the school as most staff experienced the training from the SIG. Initially, the school had high expectations of the project but realized that the demands for improvement were unlikely to be met in the timescale given.

> I think I had high expectations in terms of the groundwork that would be set for later improvement. I think the project, if you look at the people who were looking at it externally, were expecting more improvement from more of the schools within the timescale of the project.

The Head feels, however, that the school was fortunate to be part of the project.

> I think we've been in a sense lucky that the project has caught us at a time when we were probably going to improve and has probably accelerated that improvement. It hasn't accelerated it through actual content. The culture which says we're all willing to learn, that learning school culture, has certainly been developed.

The Head feels that the full impact of the project is unlikely to be felt for a few years as the school opted to invest in those aspects of OCTET that were longer term and more sustainable.

> I mean decent well-grounded development – and resisted the kind of 'quick fix' things, because they weren't really what we wanted, I don't think there were many quick fixes that we wanted to do and there were some things that didn't work for us.

The Head feels that the staff training was one of the crucial keys to success along with a greater focus and understanding about learning. 'The SIG training absolutely fabulous. Fabulous all the way through.

Highly expensive in terms of staff time, and crucial that we got the right mix of staff. I think we did'. The school deliberated for a long time about the composition of the SIG as they felt it important to get it right.

> I think some other schools hadn't got the same focus. They weren't having the same expectations of their SIG or they were in a different place to us. I think that they struggled a bit partly because of the people that they chose for the SIG. For me I think it was very well defined what the SIG should be like and I didn't have any quarrel with which staff should be on the SIG. But I know that some other heads were very concerned that they hadn't been given the right brief for what the SIG involved and was expected to do.

The ICT strand of the OCTET project within the school proved to be more variable in terms of its impact. The data processing part of it was helpful to the school but essentially it confirmed what the school already knew.

> They told us about things we were already doing and although it forced us to be a bit clearer about collecting the data and be a little bit surer about having all the data available to us like Key Stage 2 stuff, we were still, and still are, utterly dependent on the outside world for that. However hard we try, we can't get all of the data on all of our Years 7 to 13 from all of the various schools that come to us, or it comes in a variety of different formats. It's not yet simple data transfer and it feels like it should be.

The other major disappointment was the video conferencing element of the project as this simply failed to materialize.

> I think that the ICT developments overall have been hampered because of the reason that ICT developments are generally hampered. If you don't have an ICT expert in your team driving it forward, then you don't know what to do and the technical difficulties get in the way.

The Head feels that there was a need for a common management information system in all of the schools very early on to manage the data. This was partly what the project attempted but as the Head reflects:

> I would have put that into each school and said 'OK right we've now got a common way of operating the data.' If you do that to a school you disrupt it enormously because it depends on its data. That's why I'm saying six months in advance you need the team that puts it in and makes it work. It needed more input into the IT part than I think people thought it was going to.

This aspect was disappointing for the school because the ICT dimension opened up all types of possibilities for data analysis and transfer, both within and across schools.

The SIG has been a major success at the school and has effectively driven change and development forward. The group is well respected by other teachers and there is a genuine feeling that they have made a difference to the school: 'I think the SIG as a vehicle for school improvement is absolutely stunningly clever. It's subtle at loads of different depths.' In addition, the CAT data has helped the school enormously as prior to the project this data was not utilized: 'We'd never used CAT before and I wish we had. For us CATs data has been fundamentally important. If you said "What's OCTET?" then you'd get CAT and SIG as being the things for us that are OCTET; that's what most people will identify.' The Head feels that the combination of the SIG and the CAT data has increased the school's capacity to deliver high-quality teaching. In addition, the project has built capacity both within the school in terms of appointing new people like a data manager and crucially within faculties by giving teachers time to meet together.

Impact

The impact of the project is most identifiable through the SIG activity. However, as the Head reflects, it is difficult to measure impact in other areas such as culture and staff relationships. These areas have been affected by OCTET 'but their impact is harder to locate and harder to tie together'. The school would embark on the project again, if given the choice, but would opt to do things in a slightly different way.

> There are probably things I'd be clearer that aren't going to work for us, for example, the reading project. We were making decisions about all sorts of things it's that I probably would have said 'No' though we went into it very, very strongly and we put in decent quality resources and a quality teacher. The outcome for us was a negative.

It is clear that with the SIG there was a shared determination to make it successful. While its early successes weren't strong enough to keep it going itself, the deeply held view that it was the right way to go ensured that it was given the time and support for it to develop and make a difference.

It was probably my and Beverley's deeply held belief that this was the right way to go forward, that this was something new and this was something different. We were going to support it. We were going to change the way the school worked so that this was a central part of the school. That wasn't because we suddenly saw success. It was because we believed very, very strongly in it and that was the kind of leap of faith that you have to have at times.

The impact on the school has been gradual but the Head feels that the school culture is now more positive and that staff are feeling motivated. There is now 100 per cent turn out for the INSET and a general feeling that it's absolutely fine now 'to talk about learning'. The work started in the project is now planned to continue through SIG 2 and 3 and other new developmental work. The school has a strong sense of direction and clear plans about future developments and innovation. Through the project the school has learnt to be more critical of suggested changes. Teachers are more likely to ask 'Do I want it at all and then do I want it like that?' or to say 'Look, there's too much going on.' The Head feels that the project has forced the school to be really clear about expectations and to assess whether set expectations are realistic or not.

Reflections

On reflection, the Head feels that not being a member of the SIG meant that he 'lost about 80 per cent of what they did'. While the SIG reported back frequently, there was a sense in which this form of feedback simply couldn't reflect the depth of learning acquired.

They reported to me as a group initially but it gradually got to the stage where it was much more a kind of consultative role. The SIG would ask what I thought of a particular aspect or development they were considering. I would agree or not, really at an intuitive level. We were gradually developing a discussion at a professional level.

One of the major achievements for the school has been the fact that the SIG designs and delivers INSET that is well received by staff. The school changed the INSET programme to twilights rather than INSET days where four twilights equals one day: 'These twilights are really quite intense sessions where the SIG is delivering and other people are responding, sometimes the teaching material they've produced, sometimes the resources the SIG has given them.' As a result teachers are now working on their own action research projects

Two other major achievement for the school was getting a data manager in post and 'getting her working on the kind of things that we wanted to work on', and 'sticking at the project overall and managing all of the things that were going on'. The school has also changed its lesson observation schedule to look specifically for the SIG impact and data impact in lessons. Looking back, the Head feels that time to think and plan before the project started would have been useful.

> I would have liked a six-month gap so that we could set up a bit more of the infra-structure that we needed to be able to get best value from it. I would have liked to have the video constantly running so that we could have had a closer network of the headteachers and the schools and there's things that I wanted to try out that we haven't been able to try out, simply ... my science teacher teaching William's kids, for example. We could compensate for Phoenix's staffing difficulties.

On reflection the Head feels that he should have appointed someone to manage the project and its various elements: 'I was trying to manage too much of it myself and it just about worked. But probably something like the ICT bits probably would have been better had I not been involved with it because it was frustrating when it did not work properly.' The Head also feels that paired schools or trios of schools doing certain projects and reporting back on would have been more useful than trying to move all schools at the same pace and at the same time. In addition, more interaction with the heads' group was considered something that would have been very beneficial.

> I would have liked to have had a couple of days in each school with all of those heads doing some decent analysis of what was really going on. And I think we got a lot out of when we did a little bit of that at the beginning because seven heads peering round a school is a pretty powerful group. They're going to see a lot of what actually goes on. I think that was a missed opportunity in terms of the power of the group of heads to actually effect change within a school.

The school has improved considerably in the last two years and there has been a positive impact on behaviour and the learning culture: 'I think we're also clearer about what are the next steps that we need to take.' Teachers are very positive at the school as they recognize that they're getting quality INSET and 'they're getting it from people that are recognized as good practitioners within the school, and I think they are positive about the need for change'. The Head feels that staff are not always confident about what those changes are and what they look like: 'But there aren't people talking about significant overload at Whitefield. I think we've also had a behavioural improvement of some significance with the kids over the last three years, which ties with the OCTET in terms of timing.' Staff have seen positive gains. The Head feels that it also very positive that the school is at the forefront of change. Teachers generally feel motivated and willing take risks: 'It is unlikely that someone's going to say "no we can't do that" because instead they say "well, how do we do that then?"' The students have reported back in their own ways, 'in the same kind of positive sense about this is a much better school to be in and it's a much better place to be in'. The school is much clearer about expectations; the school is about learning. This is a much clearer message to students:

> One of the things that I've noticed very strongly is that new students who come in are much, much more quickly moved into the culture of what Whitefield is about (which is learning) than they were before. We used to have to spend a lot more time on induction and training people and they'd give us a lot more trouble. We can now take in new students and they're much less disruptive and disturbing on the rest of the school than it was in the past. I think that's because it's much easier to know what it is you're supposed to do in this school as a student.

The Head feels that the OCTET project has provided a harder edge to pupils' learning. There is a greater belief that 'you can make kids better'. One of the main challenges facing the school is keeping good processes going 'even when you teach students who don't need those processes. If you work as hard as we do at Whitefield in a less challenged school you end up excellent. I think Whitefield is excellent, it's just that we are unconventionally excellent!'

Reflecting on the other schools in the project, the Head feels that they share a natural turbulence in which the schools are being churned around by factors that aren't really within your control. Another common feature is the constant pressure from exam results/league tables/external expectations/statements that 'you're not very good are you and you can't be, because we can prove it. There's a constant challenge over intake and the ability to manage your own destiny in terms of the features of the intake. You are constantly challenged by the massive difficulties that there are because of the variety of needs that the students have.' However, despite some similarities, the Head feels that the schools are very different places to work and that different approaches to improvement will be required at each one.

In terms of advice to other schools about improvement, the Head feels that first, it is important to have a very clear idea about where you're going 'so that you can identify what you do want to help you and what you don't want so that you can say yes or no and that you can manage the external and the internal forces for change'. Second, there needs to be a collective recognition that schooling is fundamentally about learning: 'School is not about social work, it's not about being a hospital, it's not about all those other bits and pieces, though occasionally you have to do some of that.' Third, it is important to take risks in order to move the school forward. Fourth, it is important to have a good mix within the management team – 'It's got to be a mix of different strengths to trade off creativity with actual practicality.' Finally, there is the need for systems and procedures to be working properly: 'Good systems and structures, and once you've got that going you're then free to think about the work' – supporting learning.

In the future the Head sees exam results increasing in terms of the percentage of the five A*–C GCSE grades along with the Key Stage results, value added and the sixth form results. 'I think that we'll be much more the kind of federation, linked with other schools in terms of development and I hope jointly responsible for each individual school's actually achievement and improvement so I can see two or three schools being linked together working on their own improvement.' The Head feels that the quality of teaching and learning will get better and that use of data will improve:

> I think it will be live lesson-by-lesson data that's being fed in and I suspect some of the choices and decisions that are made will be made by the IT software rather than by me and the management team and the other people who are looking at the actual data itself.

The Head's future priorities are 'teaching and learning, getting the school full and stable, getting kids involved in their learning and having an expectation of their right to be taught well'. The Head anticipates that pupils will have much more responsibility for what they learn and how they learn.

In terms of lessons about school improvement, the Head is clear that there needs to be some kind of team to generate the capacity for improvement. There has to also be the recognition that people matter a great deal in the improvement process: 'I've probably learnt that by experience and actually didn't spend enough on the people – the people capacity.' It is also important that communication channels are opened up and that there is a no blame culture: 'Allow people to make mistakes – expect people to make mistakes but hold them accountable for what they do then after that but don't hold them accountable for their mistake – that's just pointless, it's happened, it's gone, just learn from it.' It is also essential to get the right person leading improvement and the Head notes:

> It's about tying the improvements to things that you want to do – not to someone else's agenda – do your own thinking about it and where do you want to go and probably whatever route you choose will be OK but do it. This is not a complex, a complicated science, it's about having good strong beliefs, good strong background and not being unshakable, being willing to listen but also being clear about, actually, what I want is I want kids to learn better. I want schools to operate better as schools.

Part 3
Lessons and Reflections

11 Leading and Improving Schools in Challenging Circumstances

Introduction

No one close to schools in challenging circumstances would ever think that leading them is an easy task. The work of these school leaders is hectic, fast-paced and demanding. However, it is well-known that school leadership plays an unprecedented role in determining a school's success and there is a very strong belief in the ability of leaders to promote and generate school improvement. This is reinforced in the research literature, which consistently emphasizes the powerful relationship between leadership and school development. Hallinger and Heck (1998) report that heads have an indirect, but highly measurable effect on students' achievement. The dominant message is unequivocal – effective leaders exercise an indirect but powerful influence on the effectiveness of the school and on the achievement of students (Leithwood and Jantzi 2000).

The research evidence consistently demonstrates that the quality of leadership determines the motivation of teachers and the quality of teaching in the classroom. Based on a series of comprehensive and systematic reviews of the literature across all types of schools, Hallinger and Heck (1996) concluded that the effects of school leadership on pupil outcomes were educationally significant – accounting for a *quarter* of the variation in student achievement across schools explained by school factors. In summary, the contribution of leadership to school effectiveness and school improvement is significant. Yet, with some important exceptions (e.g. Barth *et al* 1999; Borman *et al* 2000; Harris and Chapman 2002; Leithwood and Steinbach 2002), the contemporary school improvement literature has not been overly concerned with leadership in schools facing difficult or challenging circumstances. However, within schools that are improving in difficult or challenging circumstances, the quality of leadership has consistently been shown to be a major contributory factor (Hopkins 2001 and Reynolds 2001).

The breadth of data collected to inform the 'Heads' Tales' provides an important source of evidence about the leadership styles and qualities of the heads in the OCTET schools. It provides a basis for making some generalizations about leadership practice in schools in difficulty. First, their accounts revealed that of central importance was the cooperation and alignment of others to their set of *values and vision*. The heads communicated their personal vision and belief systems by direction, words and deeds. All of the heads in OCTET had chosen to work in a SfCC. Their vision and values emanated from a core belief in the ability of all children to learn and in the school's potential to offset the effects of disadvantage on student performance.

Second, the data showed that the heads' vision was shared both within and outside the school. Through a variety of symbolic gestures and action, the heads were successful at aligning staff, parents and students to their particular view of what the school stood for and how it should operate. They had a great optimism around learning and all subscribed to the view that within their school there was huge potential for student growth and development. They respected others and treated each person as an individual. They trusted others and required trust from others. They recognized the need to be actively supportive, caring and encouraging as well as challenging and confrontational when necessary.

Third, vision was an inherent part of their *leadership relationships* in the sense that it helped them communicate a sense of direction for the school. The visions and practices of the OCTET heads were organized around a number of core personal values concerning the modelling and promotion of respect (for individuals), fairness and equality, caring for the well-being and whole development of students and staff, integrity, and honesty. It was clear from everything said by the heads that their leadership values and visions were primarily moral (i.e. dedicated to the welfare of staff and students, with the latter at the centre) rather than primarily instrumental (for economic reasons) or non-educative (for custodial reasons). Their values and visions both constructed their relationships with staff and students and were constructed within them.

In short, the OCTET Heads displayed people-centred leadership in their day-to-day dealings with individuals. Their behaviour with others was premised upon respect and trust and their belief in developing the potential of staff and students commonly held. Their ability to invite others to share and develop their vision was frequently commented upon by staff and students alike. Alongside these qualities, however, were examples of heads being firm (in relation to values, expectations and standards) and, on occasion, taking very tough decisions, for example initiating competency proceedings against teachers who consistently under-performed. These heads did not gently cajole staff and students towards success but recognized that balancing pressure and support while building positive relationships was of prime importance. In many respects the way they interacted with others was the common denominator of their success. The human qualities they possessed enabled them to lead others effectively and to establish confidence in others that their vision was worth sharing. Their data also revealed a number of key leadership themes.

Leadership themes

Distributing leadership

All the OCTET heads adopted highly creative approaches to tackling the complex demands of implementing multiple changes. The decision to work with and through the SIGs was a common response to the management of change. The heads used a number of strategies for bringing out the best in staff. In addition to formal staff-development opportunities, their strategies included: the power of praise; involving others in decision-makin; and giving professional autonomy. Although the heads tended to concentrate on teaching staff in the first instance, they used similar approaches when dealing with support staff, governors, parents and students. All the OCTET heads invested in others in order to lead the school. From the perspectives of others, the overarching message was one of the Head building the community of the school in its widest sense, i.e. through developing and involving others.

Heads in OCTET schools consistently highlighted the importance of possessing a range of leadership strategies to address the diverse sets of issues and problems they faced. They also emphasized the contingent nature of many of the decisions they made and how different leadership strategies would be used in different contexts. The majority of schools in OCTET had at some stage faced the possibility and reality of special measures or serious weaknesses. The heads commented upon the importance of careful planning for the inspection. They all acknowledged that they adopted a more autocratic leadership style during the pre-inspection phase. This included paying special attention to issues such as policy implementation and consistent standards of teaching (Chapman 2002). During various inspections from HMI and OfSTED, the heads adopted a more supportive leadership style in order to assist staff through the process. All the heads took this role very seriously and consciously demonstrated high levels of emotional responsibility towards their staff during the inspection period. In particular the heads emphasized that while they had a broad set of values they adhered to, they did not consider this to be a fixed leadership approach. They felt strongly that they could switch to a leadership style that suited the situation and could behave in ways that did not reflect their core beliefs, if necessary.

Leading learning

For the OCTET heads, effective leadership was centrally concerned with building the capacity for improved teaching and learning. The heads were quick to dispel the 'cultural deficit' notion prevalent in many SfCCs, and were committed to the belief that every child can learn and succeed. They made decisions that motivated both staff and students and placed an emphasis upon student achievement and learning. The heads talked about creating the conditions that would lead to higher student performance and they were deeply concerned about the welfare and the educational experiences of minority children. They set high expectations for students, emphasized consistency in teaching practices, provided clear rules about behaviour, and stressed discipline. Their developmental focus was on improving the quality of teaching and learning. In this sense, they were instructional leaders as the emphasis was upon student attainment and achievement. The heads created learning opportunities for both students and teachers. They focused their strategic attention upon the classroom and engaged staff in dialogue about teaching and learning issues rather than issues of behaviour or classroom management. They were able to make clear links between their core values and their vision for improved student achievement and learning.

Investing in staff development

A principal concern for the heads in the OCTET project was one of maintaining staff morale and motivation. In a number of the schools staff morale had been low and individual self-esteem had been eroded by successive criticism of the school. Consequently, the heads consistently and vigorously promoted staff development, whether through in-service training, visits to other schools, or peer support schemes. It was noticeable also that such development did not only focus upon needs which were of direct benefit to the school but also those which were of direct benefit to the individual. The development needs of non-teaching staff were also included. The emphasis heads placed on the continuing development of their staff was an endorsement that teachers were their most important asset and that, particularly in difficult times, it was important to maintain their own sense of self-worth by valuing them. Consequently, they were highly skilled at using a combination of pressure and support to promote the efforts of teachers, particularly when working with the most difficult students. They encouraged teachers to take risks and rewarded innovative thinking.

The OCTET heads set high standards for teaching and teacher performance. The focus and emphasis upon improving teaching and learning was common across all schools. In most cases, time was provided to allow teachers to meet to discuss teaching approaches, and they were able to observe each other teaching. In addition, teaching performance was monitored and individual assessments made. Poor teaching was not ignored or tolerated within the schools. Where it did exist, it was challenged and strategies were agreed for improvement. Where this did not occur, the necessary steps were taken by the headteacher to deal with the problem. In the majority of cases, a combination of support, monitoring and an individual development programme addressed the problem of poor-quality teaching. For the OCTET heads, effective leadership was about capacity building in others and investing in the social capital of the school.

Relationships

The OCTET heads were good at developing and maintaining relationships. They were considered to be fair and were seen as having a genuine joy and vibrancy when talking to students. They generated a high level of commitment in others through their openness, honest and the quality of their interpersonal relationships. The heads engaged in self-criticism and were able to admit to others when they felt they had made a mistake. They placed a particular emphasis upon generating positive relationships with parents and fostering a view of the school as being part of rather than apart from the community. Stoll and Fink (1996) describe 'invitational leadership' as a form of leadership where leaders place a high premium upon personal values and interrelationships with others. Heads in OCTET did reflect many of the dimensions of invitational leadership. They placed an emphasis upon people rather than systems and invited others to lead. It was clear that while they possessed a range of leadership strategies to address the diverse sets of issues and problems they faced, at the core of their leadership practice was a belief in empowering others.

Community building

A distinctive feature of schools that are improving is how far they work as a professional learning community. Within many of the OCTET schools a climate of collaboration existed and there was a commitment among most staff to work together. However, this climate was the result of lengthy discussion, development and dialogue among those working within and outside the school. It was deliberately orchestrated through the provision of opportunities to build social trust. This included providing opportunities for dialogue between staff and parents. The heads emphasized the need to establish an 'interconnectedness of home, school and community'. This also involved adopting a multi-agency approach to problem-solving and to understanding the wider needs of the community. The implication here is that schools cannot operate in isolation from other agencies or the communities they serve.

Recent research has reinforced the importance of school leaders connecting with the community and hearing and taking account of parent (and student) voices (Chrispeels, Castillo and Brown, 2000).The heads in this study were acutely aware of the need to engage with their community. They visited homes, attended community events, communicated regularly with the parents about successes and engendered trust by showing genuine care for young people. They understood the forces within the community that impeded learning, they were aware of the negative forces of the sub-cultures and they listened to parents' views and opinions regularly. The heads tried to create integral relationships with the families in the communities they served. They recognized that 'family, school and community relationships directly affected student outcomes', hence the need to connect with the community was of paramount importance to the success of the school.

It was generally acknowledged by the OCTET heads that while local conditions varied considerably, the prevailing socio-economic conditions remained an important factor directly affecting the school's potential to improve. While the schools did not embrace the prevailing socio-economic conditions as an excuse, they like other schools facing challenging circumstances recognize that the disadvantage faced by the pupils who attend their school inevitably affects their subsequent aspirations and attainment. It was also clear that changes in the external environment could influence the school's performance both positively or negatively. In short, the social mix of the school affected the school's potential to raise pupil performance and attainment. In some of the schools deliberate efforts had been made to regain the confidence of parents and to improve the reputation of the school in the local community. It was clear that some of the OCTET schools had been losing pupils to other schools considered 'better' and that this was largely due to strongly held misconceptions about the school.

The heads were also highly responsive to the demands and challenges placed upon their school by other external forces. SfECCs are often in receipt of much more attention and intervention from the district and central government level than schools in more affluent circumstances. The schools in OCTET were under constant scrutiny and pressure to implement numerous innovations and interventions. The heads saw their role as protecting teachers from unnecessary intrusion or burdens by acting as gatekeepers to external pressures. While there were innovations and new initiatives at each school, these had been carefully selected to ensure that they would enhance the development programme of the school and would not simply compete for teachers' classroom time and energy.

Leading improvement

The data suggests that leadership within schools in challenging circumstances takes two forms. The first is concerned with the implementation of policies and initiatives aimed at addressing structural concerns within the school. The second is concerned with cultural change and development where leadership has a transformational intention and quality. The OCTET heads displayed both kinds of leadership and had instigated many changes and deployed many strategies aimed at improvement.

They had deliberately and carefully selected key areas for development and change.

The majority of schools in OCTET were located in positions that meant that their immediate surroundings were often very poor. A number of schools were located on council estates or in inner-city contexts that presented a run-down and, at times, hostile school environment. The physical condition of the majority of the schools was initially very poor with leaking classrooms, broken windows, graffiti-covered furniture and litter-covered corridors. Consequently, one of the first actions taken by heads was to improve the immediate environment in which students and staff worked. Resources were allocated to painting and repair work, to new furniture, to a new reception area, to display boards and refurbishment of the staff room. Emphasis was placed on litter removal and students were given the task of sanding down desks to eradicate graffiti. This strategy had a symbolic and real purpose as it demonstrated to staff, students and parents that the school was changing and improving.

The heads acknowledged that, at some time, the quality of the relationships between staff and also between staff, students and parents had not been at an optimum. In some cases relationships had deteriorated over time, resulting in a negative culture within the school characterized by low expectations and a high degree of mistrust. Therefore the heads invested a great deal of time in creating opportunities for more positive relationships to be developed. For staff, opportunities were provided to work together, to work across teams and within teams, social events were organized and staff development activities took place which included the expertise and involvement of those within the school. For students, staff–student committees were organized, student councils were established, lunch-time and after-hour clubs were set up and trips were organized. For parents, there were evening classes and 'drop in' sessions, all parents' evenings included a social component and there were more opportunities created to give parents positive feedback and to invite them into the school. An emphasis was placed upon breaking down social barriers and creating a climate within school where staff, students and parents had more opportunities to talk.

There are often low expectations within SfECCs of what students can achieve. Many reflect a cultural deficit notion of schooling and expect little from the community and little from the students. One of the central tasks of the leader faced with low expectations from staff and students is to generate belief in a culture of improvement. A first step in achieving this is to set clear expectations with students and staff, to share a vision of improvement, particularly with students, and to re-affirm this on a regular basis. Students, staff and parents need to know what the school has to offer them and what part they play in its development. By setting clear expectations, creating a vision and sharing this with others, the possibility for improvement is significantly enhanced. The heads were able to establish a more positive climate for learning within their school by 'talking up' the school, setting clear expectations (e.g. on behaviour, truancy, attendance) and encouraging respect for others. They imparted a sense of urgency for maintaining high academic standards and exerted pressure upon staff and students to excel.

Within SfCCs there has often been a lack of attention, emphasis and investment in staff development because of other pressures. The erosion of professional confidence and capability can, however, be a major barrier to improving schools in difficulty. In many cases, teachers feel de-valued and de-skilled, particularly if the school is in 'special measures' as teachers can become the prime focus of blame. It is important therefore that the leadership within the school ensures that teachers have the time and opportunity to collaborate. There need to be opportunities for new approaches to professional development such as mentoring, coaching and peer review. Where teaching practices are poor, improvements can be achieved simply through investing in forms of professional development and collaboration that raise teachers' self-esteem and acknowledge that they have important dimensions of their work that they can share. Providing groups or teams of teachers who have not worked together before with a specific task or an area for improvement has been shown to result in benefits, not only to the school but also to the individuals involved.

Schools that find themselves in difficulty can be subject to a wide range of external interventions that can compete for time, energy and resource. The demands of numerous initiatives can prove to be counter-productive in securing school improvement, particularly in schools where there are additional problems of social disadvantage. One way of rationalizing and focusing improvement efforts is to locate them strictly in the area of teaching and learning. Teachers in SfCCs need to acquire skills to be successful with students with particular sets of needs. They need to use a variety of teaching approaches to ensure that all children have access to learning in the most efficient and effective manner. It is also important that they provide opportunities for student-initiated and student-directed learning activities and that teachers relate instruction to practical and meaningful student experiences. By providing staff development opportunities that focus directly on effective teaching strategies and approaches, the possibility for improved teaching and learning is enhanced. Additionally, by placing a consistent and continual emphasis on teaching and learning, it is more likely that improvement at classroom level will occur.

Schools in difficulty are often located in communities of extreme poverty and deprivation. As a consequence they have to deal with problems that are a by-product of the socio-economic context in which the school is located. Indeed, the school may be viewed with mistrust and suspicion by the community. It may be seen as having relatively little to do with the lives and aspirations of those within the community it serves. A main task of the leadership of SfCCs therefore must be to build bridges with the outside community and to form relationships with families that extend beyond just getting them into the school. Schools in difficulty that are improving have a strong desire to get parents involved in the educational process. Community and families are perceived as assets that should be capitalized upon and integrated into the school in a manner that values and seeks their contribution.

Schools that have built solid and lasting links with the local community are more likely to gain their support and loyalty in difficult times. This means providing opportunities for parents to come in to school, to talk to teachers, to use the facilities and to see the school as a resource for them and their children. It means breaking down traditional barriers between the school and the community by seeking ways to integrate and involve parents in school life. It is important that schools celebrate and value a diversity of languages and cultures as community assets and that these are seen as being of intrinsic worth. Also, they must openly support educational equity and excellence for all students.

One of the main difficulties facing SfCCs is recognizing that there is a problem and knowing how to deal with that problem most effectively. For many schools in difficulty a culture of denial dominates, preventing meaningful change from taking place. One way of breaking this cycle is to put in place robust evaluation mechanisms that highlight strengths and weaknesses. By providing an internally driven means of diagnosing developmental needs, the possibility of change in increased. If staff recognize that evaluation mechanisms and data-gathering offer them powerful ways of planning development and change, they are more likely to use the information for developmental purposes.

As highlighted earlier, the research on improvement in schools in economically deprived areas is still relatively limited. However, the evidence from the OCTET project would suggest that there are three common strands to the improvement process for such schools. These are:

- focus on teaching and learning;
- setting high expectations;
- learning community.

The improvement process

Focus on teaching and learning

A clear focus on a limited number of goals has been identified as a key characteristic of effective and improving schools (Hopkins 2001; Reynolds *et al* 2005). Connell (1996), studying schools that had moved from the category of poorly performing in New York, found that a common denominator of success was a focus on students' academic achievement, and that all had developed new instructional strategies. Teddlie and Stringfield (1993) likewise found that in ineffective schools in Louisiana heads focused less on core instructional policies than they did in effective schools. Other researchers have similarly stressed that a focus on teaching and learning is crucial, something which can be encouraged by training staff in specific teaching methods at the start of the school's improvement effort (Joyce *et al* 1999; Hopkins 2001).

Across all the OCTET schools there was consistent and relentless attention to improving the quality of teaching and learning. This was identified as the single most important factor in raising achievement. In all of the schools teachers felt that the focus or re-focusing on teaching and learning through the SIG, ICT, RML and data analysis training had been the turning point for the school as it provided the impetus for classroom change and development. It was evident that many teachers had engaged in professional development activities with the explicit focus on teaching and learning. Training days were used by the SIGs to explore different teaching and learning issues and to engage teachers in dialogue about teaching. As a result of specific training events many teachers had incorporated learning strategies into their teaching.

There was general support for the CAT data analysis and associated learning styles matching as a lever for classroom-level change and improved pupil learning outcomes. The performance data would suggest that both the SIG and the CAT data analysis have had a major impact upon teaching practices in most of the schools. It has been the focus of departmental and whole-school planning and has led to new resources and ways of working within the classroom. By using data, each school was able to identify potential under achievement and to address issues of inadequate progression on an individual pupil basis. This form of formative monitoring ensured that pupils' learning was continually scrutinized and that any problems were addressed immediately. The net effect of this was to ensure that pupils were assisted to meet their full potential to achieve and were given specialist, intensive support to do so. Data-richness has long been found to be an important component of effective and improving schools in studies in the UK, the USA and Canada. Reynolds *et al*'s (2005) study of HRS components, for example, found this factor to be strongly related to improvement. Being data-rich means that data can be turned into information then used as a basis for school and classroom decision-making (Henchey 2001).

Unilaterally, all the OCTET heads set high standards for teaching and teacher performance. Time was provided for teachers to meet and to observe each other teaching. Teaching performance was monitored and individual assessments made through the performance management system. Teachers were encouraged to see professional development as an entitlement and a means of ensuring that their teaching was of the highest quality. In summary, high-quality teaching was a consistent focus and hallmark of each school.

Setting high expectations

Many of the families served by the OCTET schools have experienced extensive periods of unemployment as a result of successive shifts in local socio-economic conditions. This has steadily eroded expectations of work or a career within parts of the community. As a consequence, low expectations prevail, with their concomitant effect upon levels of pupil performance and attainment. All the OCTET heads recognized that the only way to address low expectations was to generate a belief in a culture of improvement. The first steps in achieving this were to set clear expectations with pupils and staff, to share a vision of improvement, particularly with pupils, and to re-affirm this on a regular basis. By doing this, the possibility for improvement was significantly enhanced. The heads in this study established a more positive climate for learning within their school by 'talking up' the school, setting clear expectations (e.g. on behaviour, truancy, attendance) and encouraging respect for others. They imparted a sense of urgency for maintaining high academic standards and exerted pressure upon staff and students to excel.

In all the OCTET schools considerable emphasis was placed upon raising the expectations of staff and pupils concerning potential attainment. Common strategies to raise expectations included award ceremonies, celebratory events and reward schemes. Every opportunity was seized upon by the heads to remind pupils and staff that high achievement was a shared expectation. Emphasis was placed on reward and recognizing achievement. There was a common view among the heads that the biggest challenge they faced was one of low expectations and a general apathy among pupils for learning. Consequently, emphasis was placed upon encouraging pupils to view the school as a place where they could succeed and that success was a possibility. Through the provision of after-school clubs, through learning mentor schemes and through additional incentives such as computers, pupils are encouraged to view learning as an entitlement and can envisage enjoying learning as a real possibility.

However, a problem faced by a number of the OCTET schools was that of teacher supply, because of general teacher recruitment and retention problems. In many cases, subject specialists in Maths and Science were difficult to recruit and there were long-term vacancies in two of the schools. This clearly affected the schools' ability to ensure that teaching was of the highest standard possible; however, it was recognized that the issue was one faced by schools in challenging circumstances throughout the country. It was noticeable that teachers who taught in these schools put in huge amounts of time and effort to work with students both within and outside the formal teaching day. This suggests that teaching in schools in challenging contexts requires teaching staff with huge amounts of commitment and energy.

Learning community

An increasing body of research has pointed to the need for schools to become learning communities, engaged in continuous improvement efforts and enquiring into both within school conditions and out-of-school developments, rather than being merely reactive to inspection or government initiatives. Such schools are open to change and experiment, and engaged in continuous improvement through enquiry into existing practices and evidence-based adoption of innovation (Joyce *et al* 1999). In professional learning communities the teachers in a school and its administrators continuously seek and share learning and then act on what they learn. The goal of their actions is to enhance their effectiveness as professionals so that students benefit. Learning schools are characterized by the presence of reflective dialogue, in which staff conduct conversations about students and teaching and learning, identifying related issues and problems (Louis and Miles 1990).

Within the OCTET schools a climate of collaboration existed among staff and there was a commitment to working together. However, this climate had resulted from lengthy discussion, development and dialogue among those working within and outside the school. It was deliberately orchestrated through the provision of opportunities to build social trust. This included providing opportunities for dialogue between staff and parents. The OCTET heads invested a great deal of time in creating opportunities for more positive relationships to be developed with staff and parents. For staff, opportunities were provided to work together, to work across teams and within teams, social events were organized and staff development activities included the expertise and involvement of those within the school. For pupils, staff–student committees were set up, student councils were established, lunch-time and after-hour clubs were put in place and trips were organized. For parents, there were evening classes and 'drop in' sessions, parents' evenings included a social component and there were more opportunities created to give parents positive feedback and to invite them into the school. An emphasis was placed upon breaking down social barriers and creating a climate within school where staff, students and parents had more opportunities to talk.

The OCTET heads believed that schools that have solid and lasting links with the local community are more likely to gain their support and loyalty in difficult times. Hence they deliberately created opportunities for parents to come in to school, to talk to teachers, to use the facilities and to see the school as a resource for them and their children. All the heads tried to break down traditional barriers between the school and the community by seeking ways to integrate and involve parents in school life. Social, sporting and charitable events offered particular points of entry for parents but evening classes and community meetings were also used to encourage parents to view the school as an important resource for the local community.

The evidence showed that the OCTET schools had deliberately selected and adopted certain strategies to secure improvement. There was evidence from internal and external evaluation and inspection data that the strategies adopted by the schools had impacted positively upon the quality of teaching and learning. The data also revealed that not only were all the schools determined to raise attainment but that they also placed a particular emphasis on those activities most likely to achieve this. As a result there were other activities that the schools gave less time too simply because they competed for valuable time, energy and resource that was already deployed on strategies designed to raise attainment. The selection of the improvement strategies was dependent on the particular context and circumstance of each school but in each case the consistent focus was on teaching and learning.

Commentary

While there are no 'quick fixes' for improving schools facing challenging circumstances (Stoll and Myers 1998), the evidence from the OCTET schools suggests that there are certain strategies that can contribute to raising pupil attainment within schools in the most difficult contexts. Clearly, these strategies are not exclusive to schools in disadvantaged areas, and possibly they are commonplace in other schools. However, recent research suggests that SfCC are starting at a lower baseline of improvement and that the 'fit' between the developmental state of the school and the range of strategies adopted is crucially important (Reynolds *et al* 2005). All the OCTET schools had carefully selected the combination of strategies that matched their developmental needs. In this respect, there was a highly differentiated approach to school improvement in evidence in each school. This finding reinforces the view that differential school improvement strategies are required for schools at different stages of their growth and development (Hopkins, Harris and Jackson 1997). The next chapter considers the issue of context-specific school improvement.

References

Barth, P., Haycock, K., Jackson, H., Mora, K., Ruiz, P., Robinson, S. and Wilkins, A. (1999) *Dispelling the Myth. High Poverty Schools Exceeding Expectations*. Washington: The Education Trust.

Borman, G. D., Rachuba, L., Datnow, A., Alberg, M., Maciver, M. and Stringfield, S. (2000) *Four Models of School Improvement. Successes and Challenges in Reforming Low-Performing, High Poverty Title 1 Schools*. Baltimore: Johns Hopkins University, Center for Research into the Education of Students Placed At Risk.

Chapman, C. (2002) *OFSTED and School Improvement: Teachers' Perceptions of the Inspection Process in Schools Facing Challenging Circumstances*. Coventry: University of Warwick Institute of Education.

Chrispeels, J. H., Castillo, S. and Brown, J. (2000) 'School leadership teams: A process model of team development.' *School Effectiveness and School Improvement*, Vol. 11, No.1, 20–56.

Connell, N. (1996) *Getting off the List: School Improvement in New York City*. New York: New York City Educational Priorities Panel.

Hallinger, P. and Heck, R. H. (1996) 'Reassessing the principal's role in school effectiveness: A critical review of empirical research 1980–1995.' *Educational Administration Quarterly*, Vol. 31, No. 1, 4–5.

Hallinger, P. and Heck, R. H. (1998) 'Exploring the principal's contribution to school effectiveness: 1980–1995.' *School Effectiveness and School Improvement*, Vol. 9 No.2, 157–91.

Harris, A. and Chapman, C. (2002) 'Effective Leadership in Schools in Challenging Circumstances, Final Report', Nottingham: National College for School Leadership, www.ncsl.org.uk

Henchey, N. (2001) *Schools That Make A Difference: Final Report. Twelve Canadian Secondary Schools in Low-Income Settings*. Kelowna: Society for the Advancement of Excellence in Education.

Hopkins, D. (2001) *Meeting the Challenge. An Improvement Guide for Schools Facing Challenging Circumstances*. London: Department for Education and Skills.

Joyce, B., Calhoun, E. and Hopkins, D. (1999) *The New Structure of School Improvement*. Ballmoor: Open University.

Leithwood, K. and Jantzi, D. (2000) *Distributed Leadership and Student Engagement in School*. Paper presented at the Annual Meeting of the American Educational Research Association. San Diego.

Leithwood, K. and Steinbach, R. (2002) 'Successful leadership for especially challenging schools.' *Journal of Leadership in Education*, Vol. 79, No. 2, 73–82.

Louis, K. S. and Miles, M. B. (1990) *Improving the Urban High School: What Works and Why*. New York: Teachers College Press.

Reynolds, D., Harris, A. and Clarke, C. (2005) 'Challenging the challenged: Improving schools in difficulty.' *International Journal of School Effectiveness and School improvement*.

Stoll, L. and Fink, D. (1998) 'The cruising school: the unidentified ineffective school', in Stoll, L. and. Myers, K. (eds) *No Quick Fixes. Perspectives on Schools in Difficulty*. London: Falmer Press.

Stoll, L. and Myers, K. (1998) *No Quick Fixes. Perspectives on Schools in Difficulty*. London: Falmer Press.

Teddlie, C. and Stringfield, S. (1993) *School Matters: Lessons Learned from a 10-year Study of School Effects*. New York: Teachers College Press.

12 Context-specific School Improvement

Introduction

The school improvement movement has often been criticized for ignoring powerful socio-economic influences that impact upon schools and for offering naive and sometimes simplistic solutions to complex social problems (Thrupp 2003). While, there is some substance to this position, more recently researchers working in this field have attempted to engage with the issues surrounding 'improvement' in schools in difficult contexts (e.g. Hopkins 2001; Reynolds, Hopkins, Potter and Chapman 2001; Harris *et al* 2003).The emerging evidence base points towards the difficulties disadvantaged schools face in simply getting to the starting line for improvement (e.g. Stoll and Myers 1998; Harris and Chapman 2002). High staff turnover, poor facilities, lack of resources, falling pupil numbers and constant streams of supply teachers are pressures that schools in more prosperous areas simply do not face (Reynolds, Harris and Clarke 2004). Research has also shown that factors such as geographical isolation (particularly of rural schools), selective local educational systems, weak support from some LEAs, low levels of formal qualifications in the local adult population and poor employment opportunities further compound the problem and make the extent of the educational challenge facing these schools significantly greater (Reynolds *et al* 2001).

Recent studies of improving schools in disadvantaged areas point towards the effect of 'social mix' over and above that which would be indicated by individuals' characteristics alone (Teddlie and Reynolds 2000). As Thrupp (1999, p183) notes, 'The issue of school mix highlights the powerful social inequalities in the provision of schooling.' Study after study has reinforced the fact that social background factors (SES) explain more than half the variation in pupil achievement (e.g. Rutter *et al* 1979) and illustrate how SES is related to other important factors such as staying on rates, adult employment and crime. It is clear that the performance of schools in challenging contexts remains stubbornly low, despite successive determined and well-intentioned efforts to alter the odds through targeted resources and strategic support. Initiatives such as Excellence in Cities and Education Action Zones aimed at supporting schools in disadvantaged areas have had variable success. However well intentioned these initiatives were, they have failed to offer the differentiation of response that schools required, providing instead a standard response to an improvement problem that requires greater diversity, variability and flexibility.

The extent to which any pattern of underachievement is due to the influence of the school, the community or the individual is inherently complex, making any attempt at intervention at only one level questionable. However, this is not to conclude that any improvement efforts like OCTET are pointless or that all improvement programmes are doomed to failure. The evidence would suggest otherwise. There is evidence to suggest that certain schools do improve despite high levels of disadvantage (Gray *et al* 1999; Reynolds, Clarke and Harris 2004). However, the evidence also shows that such schools have to *exceed* 'normal' efforts to secure this improvement and that performance gains are normally followed by periods of flat performance. As Elmore (2003, p11) points out, in many accountability systems 'these flat periods are seen as failures to improve and they carry heavy penalties'. In summary, success can be short-lived and fragile in schools in difficult or challenging circumstances.

Looking across various school improvement projects and programmes, even those proving to be most effective have adopted a fairly uniform approach to school development and change (Hopkins 2001). Yet the OCTET intervention demonstrates the need to embrace context specificity and to be more highly differentiated (Reynolds, Clarke and Harris 2004). However, ways of categorizing and differentiating programmes of intervention remain relatively underdeveloped. Work by researchers (Hopkins *et al* 1994, for example) highlights the need for a 'fit' between programme and the school's developmental needs. In this framework, school improvement strategies fall into three different types:

- Type I strategies: assisting failing schools to become moderately effective. Assuming that failing schools find it hard to improve by themselves, these involve a high level of external support, and strategies involve a clear and direct focus on a limited number of basic curriculum and organizational issues to build the confidence and competence to continue.

- Type II strategies: assisting moderately effective schools to become effective. These strategies do not rely as heavily on external support but tend to be more school initiated.
- Type III strategies: assisting effective schools to remain so. In these instances, external support, although often welcomed, is unnecessary as the school searches out and creates its own support networks. Exposure to new ideas and practices, collaboration through consortia, networking or 'pairing' type arrangements seem to be common in these situations.

This typology suggests that schools that are least able to improve themselves will require a high degree of external support and intervention. However, this typology fails to differentiate adequately between the different types of school that fall into the Type I categorization, a category which undoubtedly most schools in challenging contexts would find themselves. There is also an inherent danger that while strong intervention strategies might yield the quickest gains in performance within Type I schools, they might also reinforce cultures of dependency among teachers and mitigate against the possibility of generating the internal capacity for improvement. There is a real possibility of what Hargreaves (2004, p32) has termed 'the apartheid of improvement' where the strategies applied in low-performing school contexts serve to perpetuate their restricted capacity. One way of avoiding this particular trap is to begin to differentiate Type I schools further and to seek a fit between the developmental capacity of the school and the set of improvement strategies adopted. In order to achieve this, initial diagnosis of the school's growth capacity is needed. The following typology is based on the work of Stoll and Fink (1998) and Hopkins (2001). It also draws upon work by Harris and Chapman (2004) that aims to differentiate more clearly between schools which fall into the Type I or failing category.

A typology of schools in difficult contexts

This provisional model or typology draws upon the most recent empirical evidence about improving schools in difficulty (Harris *et al* 2003; Thomson 2002) and the broader research literature pertaining to schools in disadvantaged contexts (Muijs *et al* 2004). This typology uses two dimensions to delineate between different types of schools in difficulty. The first axis indicates a continuum from an individualized teacher culture to a collaborative teacher culture. The research evidence would support the centrality of teacher collaboration in securing school improvement; similarly it would indicate that an individualized teacher culture, with teachers working independently, is least likely to foster improvement or development (Hargreaves 2004; Hopkins 2004). Consequently, the degree of collaboration is a powerful indicator of a school's capacity to improve.

The second axis offers a continuum between internal and external accountability. Recent work by Elmore (2003, p. 9) has suggested that low performing schools fundamentally lack 'internal accountability', i.e. an agreement and coherence around expectations for student learning. He argues that external accountability pressure designed to improve schools in difficult contexts may have the opposite effect, actively preventing schools from succeeding. He contends that holding schools more accountable for their performance will only work if there are people in schools with the knowledge, skill and judgment to respond appropriately to the pressure to improve. External accountability policies assume that sanctions uniformly act as motivators for improvement and that all schools have the same internal capacity to improve. Such assumptions continue to thrive simply because limited effort has been made to differentiate between schools that are improving or schools that not improving in difficult contexts.

The following typology is a heuristic device for differentiating schools in 'difficult contexts'. Its aim is to demonstrate the range of internal capacity for development within this group of schools by combining two parameters that the research evidence suggests offer a powerful means of analysis. While the typology aims to include all schools in difficult contexts, it is possible that a two-dimensional analysis is too crude to adequately embrace all schools in this grouping. The intention here is to offer one lens for looking at this group of schools that highlights their very different internal capacities for change and varying levels of internal accountability. Four different school types are described.

A typology of schools in difficult contexts

Teaching culture

	Individualized	Collaborative
External	Immobile	Medium capacity
Internal	Low capacity	High capacity

Accountability (rotated, left margin)

Figure 1 A typology of schools in difficult contexts

Type A: Immobile

In Type A schools, the combination of a prevalence of teachers' individualized practice and strong external accountability measures place this school in a state of paralysis. The schools tend to exist in a state of educational crisis and are typically those found in special measures or bordering on this category because of the extent of the organizational breakdown. Within the OCTET project there were several schools that could initially be put into this category. Research would indicate that relationships within these schools are often fractured and teachers survive through individual strength or existence within small cliques. In general, professional relationships within these schools can be identified as autonomous and teacher culture as individualized. The overall knowledge and skills base within these organizations are insufficient and teachers often have few CPD opportunities. The structures in place to support the schools are frequently inefficient and ineffective.

Within this type of school any improvement approach is unlikely to succeed unless external pressure is withdrawn and efforts to create greater internal accountability are pursued. The main focus for attention within this type of school has to be securing greater trust and confidence among teaching staff. The imposition of an externally imposed and tightly prescribed programme of improvement is unlikely to succeed long term in this type of school because of its inability to respond positively and its lack of internal capacity to grow. It is possible that short, intensive interventions may reap some benefits in Type A schools but they are likely to be short-lived unless the cultural issues facing this school are recognized and addressed.

Type B: The low-capacity school

Schools that have a strong sense of internal accountability but which are still operating in a largely 'balkanized' way (Hargreaves 2004) have the basis to improve but not without significant investment in teacher development. Type B schools will be aware of their problems as their internal accountability measures will have highlighted the potential for further improvement. Again several of the OCTET schools could be categorized as Type B. Teachers within this type of school will be willing to address the problems, but research would suggest that their efforts can be unfocused or poorly supported. Within these schools, the key to commencing the capacity-building process is to invest in forms of staff development that encourage interdependence rather than independence amongst staff. This can be achieved by identifying a group of staff to lead staff development and change within the school to ensure that change is manageable and focused directly on teaching and learning. Schools in this category need to develop their internal confidence and expertise rather than relying on external input or depending upon external projects.

Type C: The medium-capacity school

These schools tend to be characterized by more positive staff relationships and ways of working together on improvement priorities. However, they still tend to be responding to external accountability pressures in their improvement or change strategies. Professional relationships in these schools indicate that the professional culture is moving towards the collaborative, with teachers regularly working together within and sometimes across departments or phases. Within these schools, research suggests that the professional development needs of individuals are starting to be met and CPD opportunities are increasing. These schools are clearly building the internal capacity to improve and carefully selected programmes of support and development focused on teaching and learning would be helpful at this stage. However, to further build capacity, the school has to develop a greater sense of internal accountability and to set its own expectations for students' learning rather than relying upon external judgement.

Type D: The high-capacity school

Schools that combine strong internal accountability measures with a collaborative school culture are those schools that will be most likely to have 'bucked the trend' in performance. The research evidence shows that teachers regularly work with each other both within and across schools. Few formal monitoring systems are needed because teachers work from a position of trust and mutual respect. As a result professional relationships within this type of school tend to be autonomous, with teachers being given significant responsibility for day-to-day and strategic decision-making. Within these schools, CPD is viewed as the key to school improvement and individuals are encouraged to explore their own professional development interests and needs. In short, these schools have the capacity to respond to external intervention approaches, which might explain why some schools in difficult contexts have found such programmes useful. High-capacity schools have the internal conditions in place to improve and to secure higher levels of pupil attainment. The main challenge for these schools will be maintaining capacity and sustaining improvement in the face of staff turnover, pupil mobility and external shifts in demographics.

Analysis

While these categories or types of schools are acknowledged to be relatively crude, it remains the case that the importance of diagnosing a school's growth state is of paramount importance if improvement strategies are to adequately and appropriately meet the needs of the school. The improvement literature pays considerable attention to the importance of the concept of context specificity, and its relationship with school improvement within the educational system but context specific programmes of improvement have been in relatively short supply. As Hopkins (2001) notes, 'authentic school improvement strategies need to pay attention to context: [the argument is] that a wider range of improvement options should be made available to schools and more intelligence used in linking improvement strategy to school need'.

The call for context-specific improvement is well established but little attention has been paid to generating the differential strategies needed to improve individual schools, particularly within the SgCC group. As Stoll *et al* (1996) argue:

What is needed to develop schools are combinations of improvement and effectiveness practices and strategies appropriate to the nature of individual schools. For a school that is ineffective and just starting the process of development, the strategies may be different from a school that has been developing for some time: the former may need an 'apprenticeship' orientation involving giving the school knowledge from outside, while the latter may be sufficiently professionally competent to develop its own good practice and the development based upon it. Likewise, the strategies would be different for an individual school at different phases of the development cycle, with beginning provision of information from outside being progressively scaled down until the school is capable of its own knowledge generation.

As was highlighted earlier, Hopkins and Reynolds (2001) talk about 'third wave' school improvement which acknowledges the importance of 'capacity building' and an appreciation of the importance of cultural change in order to embed and sustain school improvement. This work has also highlighted the importance of differentiated approaches to improvement, particularly for schools in the most challenging contexts.

The emerging research evidence concerning schools in difficult contexts (Harris *et al* 2003; Reynolds, Clarke and Harris 2004) demonstrates quite clearly that a diverse range of school level factors and characteristics is the norm. Each school within this grouping exhibits a unique organizational mix of cultural typology, improvement trajectory and level of effectiveness. Unlike effective schools, which have been shown to exhibit similar characteristics, schools in the low-performing grouping may look homogeneous but in practice exhibit very different characteristics. Therefore, it would seem important that any improvement intervention aimed at this group of schools offers some degree of differentiation.

As this typology indicates, those schools at the very trailing edge of the educational system like the OCTET schools will require significant cultural change in order to facilitate significant improvement. Both structural and cultural changes are necessary for school improvement but with schools in difficulty, unless relationships and trust can evolve positively within an organization, its internal capacity to improve will be severely hampered. Clarke (2002) labels the baseline condition 'bounded instability', where improvement is impossible without major structural change and support. Therefore, building collaborative cultures and developing professional autonomous relationships is the key to successful innovation. Moreover, the improvement strategies adopted by each type of school will be dependent on their particular growth state or type.

We undoubtedly need to know much more about improving schools in difficult circumstances and particularly about how such schools sustain improvement over time. We need to know what particular combinations of external support and internal development are optimum for generating positive change and development. Increasingly, the evidence base is pointing towards the possibilities and potential of 'learning communities' to generate the capacity for school improvement (Hargreaves 2004). Such communities offer opportunities for teachers to work together without being dependent upon external initiatives or interventions. However, much depends upon a school's internal capacity to become a learning community in the first place. It is clear that not all schools have this capacity and that those schools which would benefit most from teachers working together are least able to make this happen. As Elmore (2003, p14) points out, to meet performance targets 'schools must develop successively higher capacities' and this is achieved by generating internal accountability rather than responding to external accountability. It is clear that many accountability systems require schools with the lowest capacity to improve most through a combination of compliance and sanctions. Long term this strategy is destined to fail unless capacity-building measures are simultaneously put in place.

Gray (2004: p. 306) argues that schools that create the capacity for improvement move through three phases of school improvement: 'Catching up, consolidation and moving ahead.' He notes, however, that our ignorance about their 'starting points' serves as a block to improvement and suggests that 'We tend not to see these schools accurately because our frameworks are too limited'. Within the OCTET project this was not the case as a great deal of time was spent considering and reviewing their starting point. However, it was the case that all OCTET schools were in the position of needing to 'catch up' and to address deep-rooted underperformance.

Context-specific school improvement

As the long-term patterning of educational inequality looks set to remain, to rely on standard or standardized approaches to school improvement that combine accountability, pressure and blame to force improved performance would seem unwise. In schools in difficult contexts, this is more likely to exacerbate the problem rather than to solve it. Instead, the evidence would suggest that more *locally-owned* and developed improvement strategies are needed, which appreciate school context, best match prevailing conditions and build the internal capacity for development within the school. If the goal of raising performance in schools in difficulty is to be achieved, school improvement approaches that neglect to address the inherent diversity and variability across and within schools in the same broad category will be destined to fail.

But how is context-specific school improvement achieved in practice? Lupton's (2004) work argues that there are serious policy issues that need to be embraced to generate a greater alignment between the needs of the school and the forms of improvement interventions employed. In terms of funding, she argues that current funding mechanisms are based on measures that are too crude and therefore mask deep differences between schools. Her study suggests that some high free school meals (FSM) and ethnic minority areas may actually be more favourable environments for schooling than white, lower FSM areas and that resource allocations do not take such possibilities into account. In short, poverty or ethnicity measures may not be the optimum way of allocating extra resources to schools in disadvantaged contexts.

Another implication for policy-makers is to recognize that practice in schools in disadvantaged contexts might vary from practice in other schools and that aiming to replicate the teaching and learning processes in a 'good school' may not be appropriate or wise. As Lupton (2004, p. 35) argues:

> At the level of the school we need a better understanding of effective practice in particular circumstances, in addition to the generic practice lessons that are already available. For example, what is the optimum size of groups for pupils with emotional and behavioural needs? What are the benefits to different groups of pupils from mixed ability or streamed groups? How are parents most effective in different circumstances? At a wider level still, we may need to consider more radical models of schooling

for some disadvantaged pupils who find it difficult to learn within the standard organisational framework of a school.

A contextualized school improvement programme would need a high degree of flexibility and diversity to meet the needs of different types of pupils in different types of school. Yet as Hargreaves (2002) has suggested, there is an apartheid of professional development and school improvement which has been generated by default rather than design. He argues that while schools that are performing well enjoy 'earned autonomy' those categorized as 'failing or close to failing have prescribed programmes and endlessly intrusive monitoring and inspection' (Hargreaves 2004, p. 190). He notes that often schools in difficulty are in receipt of multiple innovations while the cruising schools with coasting teachers who ride in the slipstream of middle-class academic achievers get off scot-free (Hargreaves 2004, *ibid.*).

The implication of a contextualized approach to school improvement is to reverse this trend and allow schools in the most disadvantaged contexts the opportunities to innovate, experiment and diversify, if necessary, like schools in more favourable settings. It also implies a steady supply of well-qualified teachers who are attracted to and retained in poor areas. As Lupton (2004) notes, this will only be achieved if there are the right financial and career incentives in place to attract the best teachers to some of the most difficult teaching contexts. It is also possible that both initial training and ongoing professional development programmes need to be more carefully differentiated to prepare teachers for the particular challenges of disadvantaged schools.

While there is evidence of a general recognition of a need to move towards more context specific forms of intervention and improvement, this is happening incrementally rather than in a coherent way. As Lupton (2004, p. 36) notes, the government is inching towards contextualized school improvement policy through increasing valuable small-scale initiatives, such as OCTET. However, the pace is simply not fast enough and the scaling-up apparatus is not there. Initiatives, like OCTET, come and go without knowledge transfer or knowledge building. Each new initiative starts as if previous attempts had not existed. There are no plans to disseminate or grow the OCTET model, despite its relative success and the fact that there are elements that can be replicated at modest cost. In addition, the schools themselves felt as though they had 'only just started' when the project ended and the funding stopped. Achieving contextually specific school improvement will require a radical shift away from short-term approaches to change, from standardized approaches and from externally driven agendas. Instead, each school or group of schools will be treated as a unit of change that is socially and culturally unique, with its own starting point and distinctive set of issues and problems to which there is no automatic or easily customized solution.

Final word

School improvement is a complex undertaking for any school, but for schools in exceptionally disadvantaged areas, it presents extra challenges. In particular, improvement can be fragile and changes do not always last over time. Increasingly, sustainability is seen as critically important to all improvement efforts and, to achieve this, capacity building is central. What is noticeable about most of the OCTET schools is that they managed to maintain an upward trajectory of results following the end of the project. While the changing nature of their intake may play some role in this, the core message about raising attainment in SfECC is one of building capacity through empowering, involving and developing teachers to deliver high quality teaching, and through providing systems of learning support, guidance and assistance to ensure learning is maximized.

In addition to building personal capacity, the heads also recognised interpersonal capacity and organizational capacity as important elements of raising attainment. The heads developed interpersonal capacity within their schools by focusing on relationships. Attention was paid to developing an understanding of how individuals interact in everyday situations. They also concentrated on sharing information between staff and improving cooperation within the school. This led to the establishment of shared values and belief systems within the staff, which in turn was reflected throughout the pupil population.

Organizational capacity was also an important ingredient for success. The leaders within these schools were developing a sophisticated understanding of how teams achieve synergy and interact with each other. Building flexible, open structures that actively supported interaction and development was important. These heads also appreciated the nuances associated with organizational capacity, and they were skilled at seizing opportunities to create, develop, re-energize, merge or deconstruct teams.

In conclusion, the overarching message for schools in difficult circumstances from the OCTET schools is that while gains in student outcomes are hard fought and sustainable improvement is particularly difficult to achieve in such challenging contexts, *both are possible*. However, to succeed in these difficult circumstances requires a school improvement process that fits the individual school context and is underpinned by an unrelenting focus on improving conditions at the learning level. The resilience, capacity for hard work and continuing adherence of the OCTET heads, under the most challenging circumstances, to provide the best opportunities for pupils' learning made a significant difference to their school and its ability to improve. In all cases they had changed their schools for the better.

References

Elmore, R. (2003) *Knowing the Right Thing to Do: School Improvement* and *Performance-Based Accountability*, Best Practices Center, NGA. Harvard: Harvard University.

Gray, J. (2004) 'Frames of reference and traditions of interpretation: Some issues in the identification of 'under-achieving' schools.' *British Journal of Educational Studies*, Vol. 52, No. 3, 293–309.

Hargreaves, A. (2002) 'Professional learning communities and performance training sects. The emerging apartheid of school', in Harris, A., Day, C., Hadfield, M., Hopkins, D., Hargreaves, A. and Chapman, C., *Effective Leadership for School Improvement*. London: Routledge.

Hargreaves, A. (2004) 'Distinction and disgust: the emotional politics of school failure.' *International Journal of Leadership in Education Theory and Practice*, 27–43.

Harris, A. and Chapman, C. (2002) *Effective Leadership in Schools in Challenging Circumstances, Final Report*, Nottingham: National College for School Leadership, www.ncsl.org.uk

Harris, A. and Chapman, C. (2004) 'Towards differentiated improvement for schools in challenging circumstances'. *British Journal of Educational Studies*, Vol. 52, No. 4, 27–36.

Harris A., Muijs, D., Chapman, C., Stoll, L. and Russ, J. (2003) *Raising Attainment in Former Coalfield Areas*. Sheffield: Department for Education and Skills.

Hopkins, D. (2001) *Meeting the Challenge. An Improvement Guide for Schools Facing Challenging Circumstances*. London: Department for Education and Skills.

Hopkins, D., Ainscow, M. and West, M. (1994) *School Improvement in an Era of Change*. London: Cassell.

Hopkins, D., Harris, A. and Jackson, D. (1997) 'Understanding the school's capacity for development: Growth states and strategies.' *School Leadership and Management*, Vol. 17, No. 3, 401–11.

Lupton, R. (2004) *Schools in Disadvantaged Areas: Recognising Context and Raising Performance*. CASE paper 76, London: Centre for Analysis and Exclusion, London School of Economics and Political Science.

Muifs, D., Harris, A., Chapman, C., Stoll, L. and Russ, J. (2004) 'Improving schools in socio-economically disadvantaged areas. A review of the research evidence.' *School Effectiveness and School Improvement*, Vol. 15, No. 2, 149–57.

Reynolds, D., Harris, A. and Clarke, D. (2004) *Improving Schools in Exceptionally Challenging Circumstances*. American Education Research Association Conference, 11–16 April, San Diego.

Reynolds, D., Hopkins, D., Potter, D. and Chapman, C. (2001) *School Improvement for Schools Facing Challenging Circumstances: A Review of Research and Practice*. London: Department for Education and Skills.

Rutter, M., Mortimore, P. and Maugham, B. (1979) *Fifteen Thousand Hours. Secondary Schools and their Effects*. Boston: Harvard University Press.

Stoll, L. and Fink, D. (1998) 'The cruising school: the unidentified ineffective school', in Stoll, L. and Myers, K. (eds) *No Quick Fixes. Perspectives on Schools in Difficulty*. London: Falmer Press.

Stoll, L., Reynolds, D., Creemers, B. and Hopkins, D. (1996), in Reynolds, D., Bollen, R., Creemers, B., Hopkins, D., Stoll, L. and Lagerweij, N. (eds) *Making Good Schools: Linking School Effectiveness and School Improvement*. London: Routledge

Thomson, P. (2002) *Schooling the Rustbelt Kids: Making the Difference in Changing Times.* Sydney: Allen & Unwin (Trentham Books UK).

Thrupp, M. (1999) *Schools Making a Difference: Let's Be Realistic! School Mix, School Effectiveness and the Social Limits of Reform.* Ballmoor: Open University Press.

Index